English ⌗ Heritage

Book of
Bronze Age Britain

English ⊞ Heritage

Book of
Bronze Age Britain

Michael Parker Pearson

B.T. Batsford Ltd/English Heritage
London

First published 1993

Typeset by Goodfellow & Egan
Phototypesetting Ltd, Cambridge
and printed in Great Britain by
The Bath Press, Avon

Published by B.T. Batsford Ltd
4 Fitzhardinge Street, London W1H 0AH

A CIP catalogue record for this book is
available from the British Library

ISBN 0 7134 6801 7 (cased)
6856 4 (limp)

Contents

Illustrations

Colour plates

Between pages 96 and 97

Acknowledgements

This book would not have been possible without the discoveries and hard work of archaeologists, both amateur and professional, over the last twenty years in particular. Geoff Wainwright and Stephen Johnson asked me to write it. John Barrett, Mark Edmonds, Karen Godden, John Moreland, Niall Sharples and Roger Thomas read and commented on various drafts. Peter Dunn drew many of the reconstructions and Kate Morton drew many of the other illustrations. The following provided information, help or comments; Richard Avent (of Cadw), John Barnatt, David Breeze (of Historic Scotland), Andy Chapman, John and Bryony Coles, Jane Downes, Andrew Fleming, Claire Foley (of the Dept. of the Environment for Northern Ireland), Daryl Garton, Jon Humble, Eddie Lyons, Con Manning (of Eire's Office of Public Works), Roger Mercer, Jacky Nowakowski, Ken Osborne (of English Heritage), Julian Parsons, Francis Pryor, Colin Richards, Joe White (of Historic Scotland) and Mike Yates (of Cadw).

The following people or institutions must be thanked for their illustrations. Peter Dunn drew **2, 4, 5, 28b, 35, 50a, 58, 79, 87, 93, 94, 103, 112, 114, 115 & 117**. Kate Morton drew **12, 14, 16, 21, 22, 24, 26, 30, 33, 40, 43, 46, 47, 49, 54, 59, 60, 63, 66, 83, 86, 90, 95, 96, 97, 123 & 125**. Dawn Flower drew **17**. Somerset Levels Project supplied **1 & 6**. Paul Halstead supplied **3 & 108**. Alison Walster photographed **7, 8, 9, 62, 67, 73, 75, 76, 77 & 92**. Dave Gilbertson provided **10 & 11**. Roger Mercer provided **13a**; Peter Stone provided **13b**. Niall Sharples provided or agreed to the use of **17, 64, back cover & colour plate 15**. John Barrett agreed to the use of **18 & 51**. Charles-Tanguy Le Roux agreed to the use of **19**. Bob Bewley photographed **20, 38, 45, 53** and **56**. English Heritage provided figures **23, 25, 31, 57, 121, colour plates 1, 2, 3, 4, 5, 6, 7 & 9**. English Heritage's Central Archaeology Service provided **50, 68, 69, 70 & 91**. Corinium Museum, Cirencester, provided **27b & 32**. **28a** was drawn by Jane Durrant and provided by Cadw. Ian Hodder supplied **29**. Derrick Riley photographed **48, 55, 81, 111 & 119**. Northamptonshire Archaeology Unit supplied figures **34, 71 & 72**. **36** was drawn by Alan Braby and supplied by Ian Armit. Historic Scotland provided **37, 44, 65 & colour plate 11**. Teresa Jackman drew **52** (provided by Bedfordshire County Council). Chris Jones drew figures **61 & 105**. **63** was used with the agreement of Peter Woodward and Roger Lane. **74** was provided by Andy Lewis. Chris Boddington drew **78 & 107**. Chris Musson (for Royal Commission on Ancient & Historical Monuments in Wales) supplied **80**. The Ashmolean Museum supplied **82 & 84** (originally photographed by the late Major Allen). Alistair Barclay (Oxford Archaeological Unit) supplied **85**. Andrew Fleming photographed **88 & 89**. **98, 99 & 100** were drawn by Lysbeth Drewett and supplied by Peter Drewett. **101 & 102** were drawn by Rosemary Robertson, MAAIS. **109 & 110** were supplied by Francis Pryor. Roger Massey-Ryan drew **113**. Blaise Viner supplied **116**. **118** was provided by the Department of Archaeology & Prehistory, University of Sheffield. Frank Gardiner drew **120 & colour plate 16**. Miranda Schofield drew **120**. **124** is by David Goodger. Photographs for **15, 39, 41, 42, 104, 126, colour plates 8, 10, 12, 13 & 14** were taken by myself.

I have been asked to point out the following: **1 & 6** are copyright of Somerset Levels Project. **7, 8, 9, 62, 67, 72, 75, 76, 77 & 92** were provided

ACKNOWLEDGEMENTS

by Sheffield City Museum. **18 & 51** are from *Landscape, Monuments and Society* (by John Barrett, Richard Bradley & Martin Green), published by Cambridge University Press. **19, 63** and **106** are copyright of *Antiquity*; **63** also by permission of Wessex Archaeology. **61 & 105** are from *Rethinking the Neolithic* by Julian Thomas, published by Cambridge University Press. **80** is Crown copyright (RCAHM(W)). **28a** is Crown copyright (Cadw). **37, 44, 65, colour plate 11** are Crown copyright (Historic Scotland). **78 & 107** are copyright of *Cornish Archaeology*. **98, 99 & 100** are copyright of the Prehistoric Society. **101 & 102** are copyright of Rosemary Robertson. **109 & 110** are copyright of Fenland Archaeological Trust. The copyright for figures **113, 122 & colour plate 16** belongs to Essex County Council.

Finally I would like to thank Sarah Vernon-Hunt and Peter Kemmis Betty of Batsford for their patience and help.

Preface

European prehistory has been classified into three ages since 1836 when a Dane called Christian Jurgensen Thomsen worked out that an age of stone preceded an age of bronze which came before an age of iron. This is known as the three-age system and, with modifications, has remained with us ever since. The Stone Age has been divided into three: an Old Stone Age (Palaeolithic); Middle Stone Age (Mesolithic); and New Stone Age (Neolithic).

Since the three-age system was devised, archaeologists have realized that these divisions on the basis of technological material make little sense when attempting to discuss what actually happened in the past and how ancient communities were organized. The Mesolithic, or Middle Stone Age, was a time of gatherers and hunters, people who lived off wild resources. It makes more sense to talk about the New Stone Age as the period of the earliest farmers. Equally, the Bronze Age is a problematic category in social and economic terms. There was considerable continuity across the division between the end of the Neolithic and the beginning of the Bronze Age. The Late Bronze Age also shares much in common with the Early Iron Age. Archaeologists still use these terms but only as shorthand to refer to particular spans of time. The terms 'Neolithic' and 'Bronze Age' are no longer considered to be so helpful for our understanding of what happened. As archaeologists discovered that iron was used in the 'Bronze Age' and that metals were in use during the 'Stone Age', so they realized that the three-age system had outlived its usefulness.

We are everywhere surrounded by the past. Practically all of the British Isles has been settled for thousands of years. The traces of this occupation are often hard to find. Every successive generation has chosen, to some degree, to preserve or destroy what came before. Others have unwittingly destroyed the remains of the past by cultivating or building on top of hidden remains. Also the agencies of wind, rain and frost, as well as natural decay, have exacted their toll. Sometimes all that is left of a prehistoric settlement is a scatter of worked flints in the soil of a ploughed field. In other, more fortunate circumstances, the foundation trenches, post-holes and pits, and the remains of pottery and bone waste have survived. In the best circumstances, we might be lucky enough to find organic remains such as wood surviving in waterlogged conditions.

The sites on display to the public represent only a fraction of what has survived, with these remains forming only a tiny part of what once existed. Most of our prehistoric remains are unremarkable as places to visit. A flat field may hide a prehistoric enclosure which is only visible from the air at certain times of year. Head for some of the places mentioned in this text and you might find a featureless field, a bypass or a new housing estate. Most prehistoric sites that are worth visiting sit in splendid isolation; islands of prehistory that have survived due to some lucky accident or other. In cases like the large burial mounds, some were protected by tradition, others were simply too large to flatten without machinery, or were too far from later settlements to be worth robbing for their building stone. For the more adventurous, there are landscapes where prehistoric remains have survived over considerable areas. A good example is Dartmoor, parts of which can be explored with the Ordnance Survey 1:25,000 Outdoor Leisure Map. This shows many of the Bronze Age enclosures, field systems and house footings, but even this fine map is by no means a complete record of what can be seen above ground. At the back of this book is a list of some of the more interesting prehistoric sites which are open to the public.

There are books about prehistoric Britain, prehistoric Ireland and prehistoric Europe. This is a book which is about all of these. Ireland and Britain shared the same cultural elements for thousands of years, and the prehistoric past of one cannot be fully appreciated without the other. Equally, these islands were only separated from the rest of Europe in the physical sense. In social terms they were part of Europe and throughout this part of prehistory there were seaborne contacts in both directions. While the direction and intensity of such ventures certainly fluctuated over 4000 years, so many of the changes in the British Isles were linked to events on the European mainland.

The changing intensity of these contacts can be used as an index of social change. To write about prehistoric England would make little sense since such a concept did not exist.

Finally, the style of most introductory books on archaeology is that of the authoritative narrative, a mass of observations presented as a solid body of incontrovertible evidence. What interests me are the different perspectives for interpreting the past and the ways in which evidence may be selected to support various theories. Archaeologists are often afraid to show others that there is disagreement and controversy about what happened. Yet this is how archaeology really advances, by proposing different interpretations, critically examining other scholars' evidence and re-evaluating conventional wisdom. This is a major part of what makes archaeology fun and interesting, so I have tried to bring out some of the controversies that are around at the moment.

Introduction

This book covers both the Neolithic (the time of the earliest farmers) and the Bronze Age. However, the terms 'Neolithic' and 'Bronze Age' have been used as little as possible. In their place I have used a different sequence which describes the main social characteristics of successive eras as prehistorians see them today. The first farmers are equated with the Late Mesolithic and Earliest Neolithic (Chapter 1). The age of tombs and ancestors is the Early and Middle Neolithic (Chapter 2). The age of geometry and astronomy is the Later Neolithic (Chapter 3). The age of metalworkers and monuments, overlapping with the previous era, forms Chapter 4 and corresponds to the Early Bronze Age. The age of land divisions is the Middle Bronze Age (Chapter 5). Finally, the age of water cults is equivalent to the Late Bronze Age (Chapter 6).

The span of time covered in this book is some 4000 years, from the beginnings of farming by stone-using communities to the end of the period in which bronze was an important material for weapons and tools. In this time, people developed enormous ceremonial monuments, many to house the remains of the dead, later abandoning them to build similar monumental edifices of a different form. These were the field systems, defended hillforts and more permanent dwellings. People did not simply substitute a landscape of ritual monuments for the more pragmatic monuments of fields and farms. Rather, their ritual and spirituality were incorporated, by the end of the Bronze Age, into the dwellings in which they lived.

The face of the British Isles during this time also changed profoundly, from a forest wilderness to a large patchwork of open ground and managed woodland. Vast areas were deforested, never again to grow trees. There were also slight changes in the climate. The earliest farmers lived in a climate which was one or two degrees warmer than it is today. Small temperature differences can have considerable affects on the ability to grow crops in the uplands. Around 3500 years ago temperatures were equivalent to today, but they fell even lower by the end of the Bronze Age.

Archaeologists have continually asked themselves what kind of society existed then. We know a lot about the practices of everyday life but the evidence for political life is ambiguous. There were certainly times of considerable reorganization but there were also very long periods of stability. The early farming communities seem to have been more egalitarian than the warrior clans of the later Bronze Age. Throughout this period, ultimate authority was doubtless invested in the heavens and in the ancestors, but towards the end there were marked differences amongst the living. By the end of the Bronze Age most people inhabited ordinary round houses, but some lived in huge defensive strongholds and controlled access to resources such as bronze. These may have been chiefs, with large retinues of warriors at their command. Some archaeologists have interpreted changes from the Early Neolithic to the Late Bronze Age as the evolution of an increasingly hierarchical and class-based society. But no doubt different political transformations occurred in various regions. There may well have been hereditary chieftains amongst the early farmers, but there were probably also communities headed by councils of elders. It will always be difficult for us to distinguish between these models.

The time of the early farmers (conventionally

the earlier Neolithic) may be considered as an age of ancestors and tombs. In their monumental tombs were mingled the remains of previous generations, with all the bones mixed together. Fire and axes were used to clear areas of forest for cultivation. The axe was the supreme tool of the age and it was an important symbol for these farmers. Its manufacture and use, and its eventual disposal, seem to have been charged with magic and symbolism beyond its everyday practical purposes.

From the orientations of some of their tombs and monuments, we can see that these farmers had a basic appreciation of the cycles of sun and moon. By the Middle Neolithic (5500 to 5000 years ago) they were building monuments to the dead which incorporated a growing concern with the movements of the celestial spheres. This age of astronomy saw the construction of many enormous monuments within 'sacred' landscapes. Perhaps these communities were ruled by dynastic chieftains, who organized the large work gangs required for these tasks.

The early use of copper and bronze began in these contexts. There was the adoption of a more individualized type of pottery: beakers, probably for drinking mead, were placed in individual graves. This rise of individualism in funerary practices has been hailed as evidence for chiefdoms, but it may in fact signal their demise. Burial, or destruction, of exotic personal possessions after death may have formed part of a way of life that shunned hereditary inequality.

Large tracts of upland were divided up at least 4000 years ago. The stone circles and other ceremonial monuments of the earlier Bronze Age seem to have lost much of their importance. The latest ones were not only smaller but were concentrated in the agriculturally more marginal regions of the British Isles. Settlements became solid and semipermanent fixtures in the landscape for the first time. In contrast, the physical remains of the dead, formerly so dominant in people's lives, went backstage. An architecture of the dead was replaced by an architecture for the living. Ancestors may still have been important but their power resided in the houses and settlements of the living.

Towards the end of the Bronze Age, the sword had replaced the axe. Warfare seems similarly to have become highly significant. It was to the land and particularly to water that sacrifices and offerings were made. Large quantities of bronze weapons and tools were thrown into rivers and other watery locations. Many of the uplands were abandoned and settlements congregated in the river valleys. Concern with community defence in hillforts accompanied the profusion of weapons of war.

We still know little about this age before written records. Every year brings new discoveries, some of which dramatically alter our understanding of what happened. Our interpretations also change as a result of re-examining old evidence. The account that follows is based on advances in research made largely in the last two decades. It will soon be out of date as more evidence comes to light and as newer interpretations are formulated. The past is never fixed; it is constantly being rewritten. And we must also remind ourselves that, back in the Bronze Age, people were also 're-writing' their past through the monuments and artefacts of their daily lives.

1

The coming of the first farmers

In the spring of 1970 Raymond Sweet, an employee of the Eclipse Peat Works, discovered a plank of wood buried deep in the peat of the Somerset Levels. His discovery was to lead to one of the most significant advances in archaeology in recent years – a wooden trackway built at the time of Britain's earliest farmers. The peat works sent the planks to John Coles, a Cambridge archaeologist who had been studying the Levels for some years. That summer he came over to Somerset and carried out an archaeological excavation on the site where the timbers had been found.

We now know that the timbers formed part of a trackway that was built across the low-lying, marshy Levels, during the winter months exactly 5777 years before they were rediscovered by Mr Sweet (1). This trackway linked the Polden Hills with Westhay Meare, at that time an island surrounded by marshes. Today the Levels are no longer marshes but drained meadows. The precise dating of the trackway has been achieved by dendrochronology. The age of a tree can be gauged by the number and pattern of its growth rings. The thickness of each ring depends on the particular climatic conditions in that year, so that, over a span of fifty or more years, the variation in thickness of the rings produces a distinctive 'signature' for that period of time. From finds of oaks of different ages preserved in bogs, archaeologists have been able to fit together a full sequence of tree rings which goes back well over 7000 years. It has been possible to fit the distinctive signature of the ring sequence from the Sweet Track's timbers with the master sequence, to work out just when the trees were felled. The oak trees incorporated into the trackway were cut down in the winter of 3807 to 3806 BC. They

were probably split into timber and laid as track soon after.

Who were the builders and why did they construct trackways such as this? We are not sure of the answers to these questions but there are a number of clues, patiently gathered by archaeologists over many years under the direction of John and Bryony Coles. We cannot be absolutely certain that the builders were farmers but they used farming equipment. The wood was cut with stone axes. Someone even placed a special axe made of green jadeite by the side of the Sweet Track. A pot filled with hazelnuts was also broken there. Gatherer-hunters in Britain did not know how to make pottery and the appearance of pottery is associated with the appearance of farming. There was also a small collection of struck flint flakes strewn along the line of the track. Their broad and long blades are characteristic of the farmers' flint technology, very different from the small and delicate flints (called 'microliths') of the gatherer-hunters.

The tracks may have linked communities living on the Polden Hills with people living on the island. The trackway also provided a corridor along which people hunted the wildlife of the marsh. The Sweet Track was not an easy route to traverse. The walker had to negotiate a slippery plank less than 25 cm (10 in) wide, pegged and jammed into place between diagonal timbers. Construction of this track was not a major task, even though it ran for over a kilometre. It would have taken just a dozen people only a single day to lay it. However, the preparation and transport of the timbers would have taken much longer. Thousands of wooden pegs, planks and rails had to be manufactured, involving the selection and felling of trees, the splitting of logs and the working of timber. This required the work of at least two small communities (working in different areas of woodland at either end of the trackway) during the preceding year. The timbers then had to be assembled along the route in the weeks before the track was laid. The trackway was repaired over the next ten years but fell into disuse after that.

1 (*Above*) *The Sweet Track under excavation.* **2** *Time chart of the Neolithic and Bronze Age.*

1 RADIOCARBON DATING

Archaeologists dealing with the prehistoric period have to depend on radiocarbon dating to work out the age of sites and artefacts. The technique was developed after the Second World War and enables a date to be determined as an expression of probability within a specified range of time. Prehistoric remains can be dated only approximately, to periods within 200 years and sometimes less. Previously, archaeologists had dated prehistoric remains in Britain and northern Europe by extending chronologies based on artefact styles across Europe from Egypt and the western Mediterranean, where early written records gave some basis for dating artefacts. Radiocarbon dating revolutionized this framework. We now know that the earliest farmers were here at least 6000 years ago, over a thousand years earlier than had previously been thought.

The radiocarbon method works by measuring the decayed half-life of a carbon isotope, C^{14}, which is present in the atmosphere and is absorbed by all living matter. The C^{14} starts to decline as soon as the living matter dies (for example when a tree is chopped down). It was initially assumed that the rate of C^{14} in the atmosphere was steady, but studies of annual growth rings from the oldest tree in the world, the bristlecone pine, have discovered that there have been variable amounts of C^{14} in the atmosphere. The calculated half-life of a sample has to be calibrated against this variation. The sample itself is dated by estimating the probability of its falling within a certain period of time, normally within three or four hundred years. Within Europe, prehistoric dates are conventionally referred to as Before Christ (or BC). In other parts of the world there is a growing trend to refer to dates as Before Present (or BP). Present is taken as AD 1950, when radiocarbon dating had become established. The dates used in this book will use BC conventions. Radiocarbon dating can be applied to bones, antler and horn, timbers and vegetable matter (whether burnt or waterlogged), peat and organic matter in soils. The advantage of its applicability to common types of archaeological evidence is balanced by its relatively coarse estimations, reliable to within a few hundred years; this may be fine for those who deal in thousands of years. In contrast, dendrochronology can only be applied to well-preserved, waterlogged timbers but it does give

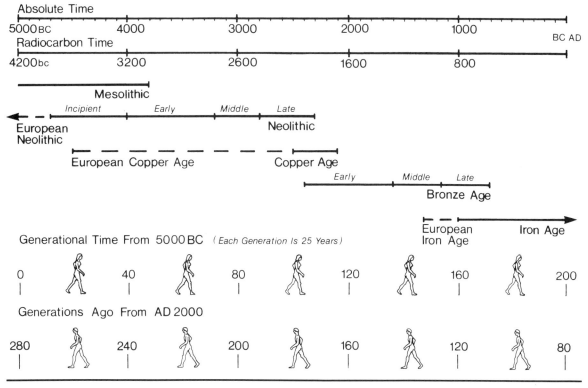

us very precise dates indeed. This is how we know, for example, that the timbers of the Sweet Track were felled over the winter of 3807 and 3806 BC.

It is always difficult working out what a thousand years – or even a hundred – mean in human terms. Perhaps the most effective way is to consider time in human generations. The conventional length of a generation is taken as 27 years so there would be just under four in a hundred years. The Sweet Track was built by people some 215 generations before us. Those of us who have traced family trees will grasp just what considerable depths of time are involved in even 20 generations.

The origins of farming

The Sweet Track was built around the time that farming communities were established in Britain. We can distinguish the remains of these farmers from those of gatherer-hunters in several ways. The first farmers used polished stone axes, pottery and a new flint-knapping technology; they raised animals and grew crops which we recognize as domesticated. These domesticates can be identified from the food remains: for instance, the bones of cattle, sheep and pigs and the charred remains of wheat and barley seeds. Cereal pollen can also be identified in peat bogs and other accumulated sediments. However, there is a controversy over just how and when farming arrived in these islands.

Farming originated in the Near East around ten thousand years ago. Local wild species of animals and grasses in that region had been carefully bred for thousands of years to improve their manageability and yield. Wild cattle, sheep, goats and pigs were probably herded and ranched, while stands of cereal were carefully tended. The domesticated animals were smaller than their wild counterparts while the grass seeds were larger. The sheep were like the modern Soay breed (3), while pigs were smaller versions of wild boar. It seems that a 'package' of all these species of animals and cereals was combined to create a farming lifestyle. Archaeologists used to say that farming had been 'invented' simply because it was a naturally better way to live, because it represented progress and development. Recent evidence has led them to question this assumption. To begin with, farming requires considerably greater inputs of labour than a gathering-hunting lifestyle. People have to work harder to clear trees and vegetation, break the ground, sow crops, control stock, prevent stock eating the crops, and harvest the crops. Equally, mobility is severely curtailed.

Whereas bands of gatherer-hunters could roam over a large area collecting food in different places in different seasons, farmers have to stay in one place to look after the stands of wheat and barley. The animals may be moved to new pastures during the year but, by and large, the only long-distance movement is through migration caused by population expansion. Labour power, far more than land availability, seems to have been at a premium for early farming communities. Women's reproductive capabilities were a key resource; the more children, the more land that could be cultivated. Farming was probably linked to a population explosion. As people became sedentary, so it was possible to bear and wean more children.

It has been suggested that the adoption of this laborious and sedentary way of life was due to necessity rather than any perception of longer-term benefits, such as the ability to store food in bad years. From the remains of earlier communities in the Near East, from the period just before the development of farming,

3 *Soay sheep, very similar to the sheep of the Neolithic and Bronze Age.*

archaeologists have inferred that they hunted an increasing diversity of animals, including those which were smaller and harder to catch. From the surviving animal bones thrown away as rubbish, archaeologists considered that people's diet shifted from the large, slow-moving mammals to smaller game such as birds and fish. It has been suggested that this was because they had hunted the larger game almost to extinction and were forced to invent new ways of catching and trapping their food. However, recent research has indicated that this 'broad spectrum' revolution in methods of obtaining food may in fact never have happened.

Theories such as this portray the earliest farmers, and their predecessors, as helpless victims of their environment, forced to alter their lifestyles due to changed natural circumstances partly of their own making. A recent theory has challenged this view and proposes that the whole process of domestication was a long-term social development in the way that people perceived themselves and their food resources as 'domesticated'.

This change was not caused by necessity but by new circumstances of living in larger groups. As food resources became more and more reliable in the Near East, so people stayed increasingly in one place. Living in large, sedentary communities brought new challenges and pressures. People had to live together as never before and find ways of co-operating as well as competing. Status and position became important concerns and were dependent on holding feasts and controlling the supply of food. People 'domesticated' themselves as well as their food supplies. New attitudes to what was meant by the terms 'culture' and 'nature', 'wild' and 'tame' may well have been embodied in the ways that their houses were built and their dead buried.

Once farming had become firmly established throughout the Near East (in what is now Turkey, Syria, Iraq, Jordan, Palestine and Israel), it was adopted by adjacent communities who acquired the domesticates. The farming package had reached the central European plains of what are now Czechoslovakia and Hungary by 6000 BC. It took only a few centuries for farming families to expand and spread westwards across the light soils to reach what is now the area covered by the Netherlands and northern France.

How and when did the farming package arrive?

There is no doubt that domesticated animals and plants had to be carried by boat from the continent of Europe to the British Isles. There are a number of options. Groups of pioneers could have set off from the continent in one-off small-scale invasions. Or people might have arrived after a long-term and eclectic mixture of contacts down the continental coast from Denmark to France. Or gatherer-hunters might have travelled by boat to the continent and brought back the animals and plants as the result of slowly developing exchange contacts. There is no answer to this puzzle, which is all the more intriguing since the earliest evidence for farming in the British Isles comes from Ireland and not from southern Britain.

The gatherer-hunters of the British Isles lived in a relatively sophisticated society. Glimpses of their way of life may be caught very occasionally where there is waterlogged preservation of the complete range of their material remains. For the clearest picture of their lifestyle, we must look at the splendidly preserved sites across the North Sea. Excavations at Tybrind Vig in Denmark have uncovered the wooden and organic remains that have often been lacking on sites in this country. In many ways this was the 'Wood Age'. They were skilled woodworkers, producing logboats and ornate, decorated paddles. They had nets and traps for fish, and beautifully made harpoons and fish spears.

Whilst gatherer-hunters lived in primitive and temporary 'benders' (huts built of branches and stakes), they were by no means isolated groups. We can find the material evidence of contact between different regions by examining their stone tools. In northern Ireland and southern England, some of their stone axes can be shown to have originated from particular rock outcrops. It appears that the axes were moved some distance from where they were made to where they were eventually discarded. A distinctive type of chert (a flinty rock used to make stone tools) has been found across most of southern Britain but it outcrops only at Portland Bill. These tools travelled long distances, presumably because they were exchanged between different communities. The stone tool kits of microlithic flints (small blades and points) also reflected regional styles, which may have corresponded to social territories.

19

People were capable of sailing far from land, as the evidence of deepwater fish in their diet shows. It is just possible that they changed to a farming lifestyle by crossing the Channel and bringing back domestic crops and animals.

When farmers reached central and northern Europe they developed a distinctive way of life. They lived in large wooden longhouses (5 m (16½ ft) wide and up to 30 m (98 ft) long) which were plastered on the outside with mud dug from ditches on either side of the house. They used pottery vessels (4), stone axes and chipped stone tools. They exploited the lightly wooded loess plateaus of northern Europe (loess is a light, free-draining and fertile soil, accumulated as wind-blown silt during the last glaciation). These were areas uninhabited by indigenous gatherer-hunters, who exploited the species-rich environments of lakesides, rivers and coasts.

When the farmers of central Europe reached the western limits of the loess plains around 5500 BC, they seem to have gone no further west for some centuries (5). In the Netherlands, Belgium and western France farming did not travel the next 100 km (62 miles) for another 500–1000 years. As well as reaching the margins of the loess, farmers also came face to face with the gatherer-hunters of the coastal margins of north-west Europe. What happened between these two groups we may never know. Sites in Holland have shown the use of imported cereals and pottery by gathering communities by 5000 BC, but the full range of domesticates did not appear until 500 years later. This time lag is also apparent in Denmark where the gathering-hunting lifestyle continued unchanged by the presence of farmers to the south until 4500 BC. The communities of the coastal fringe were gradually adopting elements of the lifestyle of the new colonists from the east. To add to the pressures of contact, the sea level continued to rise. Large areas of coastal plain, prime environments for wild food, became submerged during this time. People may have been forced partly by climatic circumstances to adjust their way of life or take up a new one.

Most archaeologists consider that the interaction and contact between gatherer-hunters and farmers must have been complex and drawn out over hundreds of years. The farming lifestyle which eventually took root in the British Isles shared elements with all the contact

4 *Early Neolithic pots found in the Somerset Levels.*

areas along the continental fringe of Denmark, Belgium, Holland and France.

The elm decline and before

Until quite recently, archaeologists and palaeobotanists were fairly certain that the beginnings of farming in the British Isles occurred around 6300 to 5500 years ago (4300–3500 BC). Within this date range (and perhaps within just 500 years) occurred the 'elm decline'. Throughout the British Isles, pollen cores of this date exhibit a marked decrease in the pollen of elm, indicating that the number of elms was dramatically reduced and, in many areas, never recovered. It has been suggested that this decline was due to the collecting of elm leaves by the earliest farmers as winter fodder for their animals. Another suggestion was that stands of elm would have indicated the lightest and best draining soils for farming and that these areas were cleared in preference to others. The trees might also have died due to debarking by cattle or ring-barking by farmers in advance of clearance. The problem with these explanations is that some 40–80 million trees must have died to produce the effects recorded in the pollen samples.

In the aftermath of the Dutch Elm disease of the 1970s, archaeologists wondered whether the Neolithic elm decline – the classic indicator of the first farmers – might not, in fact, be the result of disease carried by the elm beetle. A few years ago remains of elm beetle were found in deposits pre-dating the elm decline from

5 *A view over an early farming landscape on the loess lands of Europe, showing the longhouses built by the settlers.*

West Heath Spa in Hampstead. It was thus perfectly possible that this decline was entirely due to the beetle. But how had elm disease moved across Denmark and north-west Europe into Britain, to spread throughout the islands from southern Ireland to northern Scotland? Had it been transmitted unwittingly by human carriers of diseased wood? Or had they realized the destructive capabilities of these little beetles and deliberately encouraged their spread so as to aid forest clearance? Perhaps the elm decline was due to several related causes rather than just one. Diseased elms would have created natural clearings which could have been enlarged by human activities. Clearance led to further elm damage. For example, stripping of bark and leaf collection would have increased the incidence of infection of the trees, spread the disease and prevented elms from recovering.

6 *Another Neolithic timber trackway, known as Garvin's track, in the Somerset Levels.*

Although there were some areas where only elms declined at this time, pollen diagrams from many areas (such as the Somerset Levels (**6**), Hockham Mere in Norfolk and Ellerside Moss in Lancashire) show that trees other than elm, such as lime, oak and alder, also declined at the same time though they recovered one or two centuries later. The occurrence of occasional cereal pollen grains with these declines in tree cover has been taken as indicative of agricultural clearance. These particular moments are identifiable at specific levels in the peat cores from which the pollen diagrams are reconstructed. The peat from those precise levels can be radiocarbon dated, and for some time such dates were thought to be those of the earliest agricultural communities in the British Isles.

There the matter rested until the last 25 years, but we now have a number of even earlier dates for farming settlements as well as cereal pollen, especially in Ireland. At Ballynagilly, in Northern Ireland, a pit containing pottery and flint tools and waste characteristic

7 *A Neolithic stone axe, made in Cornwall but found north of Rotherham. (Slightly less than lifesize.)*

of farming assemblages (broad and large flakes, leaf-shaped arrowheads), was dated by radiocarbon to *c*.4700 BC. A stone tomb (a form associated with the early farmers) at Carrowmore also produced a similar radiocarbon date. Most archaeologists have dismissed the latter as coming from an uncertain context in the tomb while others consider the Ballynagilly date to have come out too early. However, cereal pollen has been recovered from deposits of the same broad period from Cashelkeelty in southern Ireland, Ballyscullion in northern Ireland and from Lismore Fields in Derbyshire. Again, the issue is clouded since palynologists (pollen analysts) are unable to distinguish between the pollen of wild and cultivated cereals. In any case, cereal pollen is not dispersed by the wind as far as other species' pollen, so the chances of it landing in bogs and other wet areas across a large region are considerably less than for the pollen of other plant and tree species. Forest clearance also took place at Broome Heath in East Anglia, on the North Yorkshire Moors and on Dartmoor seven thousand years ago. Were these the traces of gatherer-hunters or of farmers?

Gatherer-hunters and farmers

If there is considerable controversy over the presence of farming in the 500 or so years before 4000 BC, we can be sure that around that date there were communities of gatherer-hunters and of farmers living in Britain and Ireland. While the farmers often selected inland sites on light soils a hundred metres or so from watercourses, they would rarely have competed for the coastal and upland spring-head locations preferred by gatherer-hunters. Nevertheless, in certain areas such as Lough Neagh and the river Bann in northern Ireland and in the upper Thames and the Fen edge of eastern England, occupation sites relating to both have been found in the same areas or in similar locations. The evidence for integration and contact is tantalizingly ambiguous, and comes largely from Ireland. At Ferriter's Cove, on the Dingle peninsula, a flint knife (of the farmers' flintworking style) was found on a gatherer-hunting site. At Sutton, Dublin Bay, a probable cattle bone was found in a gatherer-hunters' midden, or rubbish heap. In the region around Lough Neagh farmers and gatherer-hunters must have been living in close proximity since settlements of both types and of the same date are found close together. Some archaeologists consider that these are exceptions which prove the rule that the two life-styles remained very much apart. Others emphasize that some of our best evidence for this period comes from Ireland, and it is only here that we are starting to get a clear picture of what happened.

One problem is the very small number of sites that have survived from this period. Another problem is the classification of 'gatherer-hunter' and 'farmer' employed by archaeologists interpreting the material evidence. The 'microlithic' flint-knapping techniques are considered to define the Mesolithic (Middle Stone Age) gatherer-hunters of this period and earlier (8). This microlithic tradition is very different from Neolithic (New Stone Age) flintworking associated with farmers,

8 *A group of Mesolithic flint tools,
characterized by the thin and small blades
known as microliths.*

9 *A group of Neolithic flint tools. They are
squatter and chunkier than Mesolithic flints.
(Slightly less than lifesize.)*

recognizable by the broad blades and flakes and by the polished axes (**9**). There is one exception: the gatherer-hunters of northern Ireland at this time used short and broad blades and flakes (known as Bann flakes). Archaeologists have perhaps too readily identified knapping techniques and tool types with particular groups using different subsistence strategies (ways of obtaining food). It is certainly the case that microliths rarely occur with either pottery or the bones of domesticates. But perhaps some people farmed and gathered, using a 'Mesolithic' technology in some environments and a 'Neolithic' tool kit in other circumstances. Equally, whilst microliths disappeared, there seems to have been some technological continuity in other aspects of flint knapping.

It was not just the use of pottery, domesticated food and a new flint technology that marked the arrival of farming. People's beliefs

in the ways of the world now seem to have been very different from the gatherer-hunters. They have left us with the earliest architecture – great tombs and enclosures constructed out of rocks, timber and soil. The earliest of these are much later than the first cereal pollen and many archaeologists consider that their dates of construction mark the arrival of the first farmers. Alternatively, these monuments could have been built many centuries after farming communities had become established. For half a millennium farming practices may have overlapped with gathering and hunting, before tomb-building and other engineering ventures were taken up across the British Isles.

One of these early engineering projects was the construction of the Sweet Track. Archaeological opinion about its purpose, whether sacred or secular, is mixed. Other remains from the early Neolithic have similarly forced archaeologists to consider whether we can understand their purpose in our own terms of practical utility. Equally, to interpret everything as sacred or ritual may also be wrong. We have to try to understand how their values were different from our own and how their (to us) bizarre practices might seem logical in terms of those values.

2 THE BRITISH ISLES BEFORE FARMERS

At the end of the last Ice Age, some 12,000 years ago, the climate of northern Europe gradually became warmer. This change, over thousands of years, was marked by the succession of particular ecological systems spreading northwards. Bare tundra was replaced by birch forests, which were replaced by pine woods. The pines gave way to mixed deciduous woodlands of oak, elm, lime and hazel. We have learned about past environments from the remains of pollen grains trapped in peat bogs or in ancient buried soils, where the acidity of the soil has preserved the pollen. The remains of snails and beetles can also tell us about the local conditions of vegetation from archaeological sites. Past fluctuations in climate can also be measured from samples of deep-sea sediments, by calculating the fluctuations in amounts of particular oxygen isotopes.

With the end of the Ice Age, human communities were also moving north, following the animals that they hunted and gathering edible plants and fruits. The landmasses that we call Britain and Ireland were not islands then but were linked to the rest of Europe by wide, low plains (now the Irish Sea, the Channel and the North Sea). Gatherer-hunters had reached the British Isles by 10,000 BC. As the glaciers melted and retreated, so the sea rose, covering these plains and isolating the communities on these islands. Ireland remained connected to Britain by a landbridge, which did not disappear until 5000 BC.

Six thousand years ago (4000 BC) woodland extended throughout the British Isles. There

10 *Birch/oak/hazel woodland on Oronsay, Scotland.*

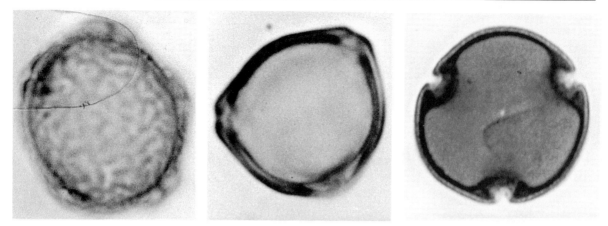

11 *Pollen grains of elm (*Ulmus*), hazel (*Corylus*) and lime (*Tilia*).*

were small patches of grassland on dry and infertile soils, such as the Breckland of East Anglia and in Upper Teesdale, but otherwise these islands were covered by forests of various types of trees, forming a Wildwood. Birch and

12 *A pollen diagram, showing the rise and fall of pollen from different species of trees, shrubs and other plants in the Neolithic and Bronze Age in the Gordano area, Bristol.*

pine predominated in the Scottish Highlands; Ireland was forested principally by hazel and elm. Open woodlands of oak and hazel dominated the highlands of England, Wales and southern Scotland, those areas which are today devoid of trees and which we mistakenly regard as 'natural' landscapes. The lime (linden tree) forests of lowland England were the most complex. They formed a mosaic of lime, hazel and oak woods with local pockets of ash, elm and beech. Alder grew in wet areas and the Fens

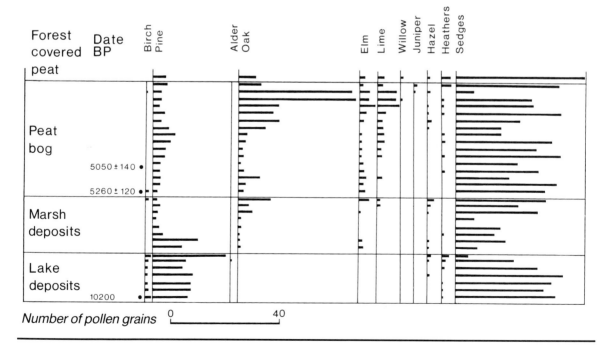

were characterized by pinewoods. The Wild-wood was composed of very diverse local woodlands which varied across the country. Much of it formed a leafy canopy some 15 m (50 ft) high, blocking light to the woodland floor. In areas like the Fens, enormous bog oaks found in the peat indicate that trees here grew straight up to a canopy at 30 m (100 ft) above the ground. Breaks in the canopy, as trees died and fell, allowed small glades to form and plants such as devil's bit scabious, bugle and cuckoo-flower to flourish. There were also edible plant foods: acorns, blackberries, barberries, sloes, crab-apples, haws and hazelnuts. Even weeds which grew in clearings could have been eaten. These include fat hen, knotgrass, annual knawel, corn spurrey, common orache and chickweed.

Red deer, roe deer and aurochs (large, wild cattle) browsed in the natural clearings. Elk inhabited marshy open woodland. Other mammals included wild boar, badger, hedgehog, woodmouse, weasel, wildcat, polecat, marten and shrew. In the rivers and coastal waters wildlife flourished: molluscs, crabs, salmon, eel, perch, pike and sturgeon were there for the taking. The sea contained seals, dolphins, whales and many kinds of fish. The bird life included cranes, storks, mergansers, lapwings, guillemots, northern divers and the flightless great auk (now extinct). There were no snakes in Ireland. Neither were there roe deer, aurochs, otters or beavers. There had been a giant Irish deer but it had become extinct before any people arrived.

Many of these animals, including whales, great auks, aurochs and deep-water cod, were taken for food by gatherer-hunters living in the coastal zones of Scotland. The only domesticate of the gatherer-hunters in the British Isles was the dog, a useful hunting aid where smell rather than sight was the key sense in dense forest. Throughout these islands these communities seem to have exploited principally two ecological zones: the lightly-wooded coasts and the highland areas of open woodland where the large mammals browsed the forest edge. They may have moved between the coastal and inland areas, or just between coastal areas, or even stayed in particular coastal locations. In some areas they may have cleared open woodland to encourage browsers. Areas of upland Yorkshire, the Lake District and Wales seem to have been deliberately cleared by burning, and hunters may have reduced parts of the Black Mountains from forest to moorland seven thousand years ago.

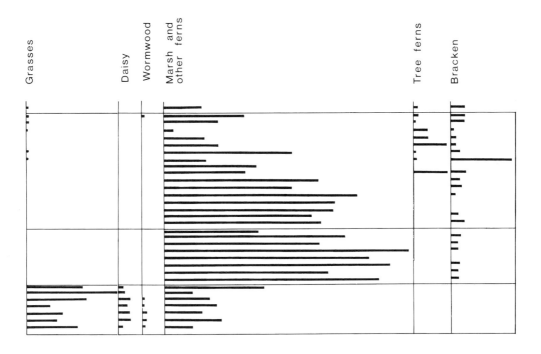

2

Tombs, territories and ancestors

In 1978 a team of diggers led by Roger Mercer uncovered a human skeleton lying face down, just outside the ramparts of a large enclosure dating to *c*.3700–3200 BC, at Hambledon Hill in Dorset (**13**). The skeleton, of a young man probably in his late teens, lay under a thin spread of chalk. He had been shot in the back; a flint arrowhead was found in a position indicating that it had entered his ribcage from behind (**13b**). His body had then been covered over by the thin layer of chalk where he had fallen. A further surprise was the skeleton of an infant crushed beneath his body. He had evidently been carrying the child and had fallen on it as he was shot. The archaeologists had uncovered a scenario of surprising detail, an ancient and anonymous human tragedy. But why had it happened?

Was the young man a thief or an enemy who had stolen the child? Was this a tug of love that ended tragically? The enclosure outside which he lay was strongly defended. He might have been killed in an attack. Was he using the child as a human shield? Or was he one of the last defenders, trying to make a run for it when all was lost?

If the enclosure had been a defended settlement, the rest of the hilltop seemed to have been used for a very different purpose (**14**). There were banks and ditches demarcating a larger enclosure which had outworks on the spurs of the hill. The ditches were not continuous but interrupted by causeways of natural chalk. In other words, they had been dug in short sections with gaps left between them. Hambledon Hill is one of a number of such 'causewayed enclosures' known from southern Britain, Denmark and France. Another recently excavated example is Briar Hill, near

Northampton, where the ditch circuits formed a complex arrangement. Some of these causewayed enclosures were defensive. At Knap Hill (Wiltshire), where the earthworks are well preserved, the ditches were interrupted by causeways but the internal bank was continuous (**15**). Also the well preserved sandmarks of an enclosure at Sarup in Denmark (**16**) indicate that timber palisades prevented access across many of the causeways. Others, such as Briar Hill and Staines, seem to have had no permanent or secure fortifications and are thought to have been ceremonial in purpose since they do not appear to have been defensible. Even the apparently defended enclosures were used for ceremonial purposes. For example, inside the Sarup enclosure archaeologists found numerous pits containing offerings of pottery, ornaments and other goods.

The ditches of causewayed enclosures were filled with feasting debris, the bones of cattle, sheep and pigs and broken pottery. There were also more macabre finds. At all levels in the ditch fills of the larger enclosure at Hambledon were bits of human skeletons. Skulls had been placed on the bottom of the ditches soon after the ditches had been dug. Most of the remains were disarticulated: they were no longer complete skeletons but scattered single bones and parts of skeletons, such as limbs and torsos. Bones from the lower part of a torso (pelvis, femur and vertebrae) were found articulated. This is the part of the skeleton which has the strongest muscle attachments and is the last to fall apart. Were these the scattered remains of victims from a battle? Probably not, since they were deposited at many different times during the slow silting of the ditches. Roger Mercer has suggested that these are the remains of the

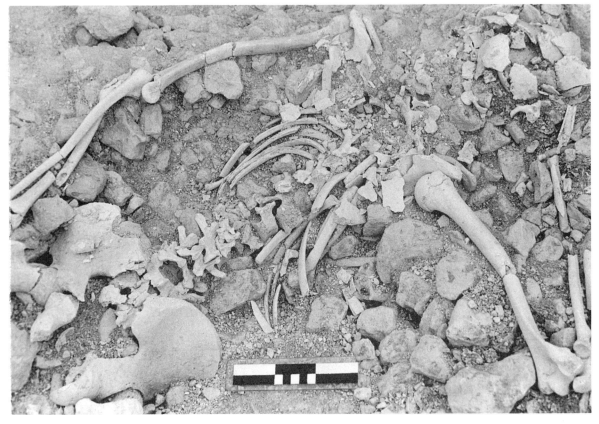

13 *The skull (broken some time after death), ribcage and pelvis of a young man, lying where he fell in the ditch of the causewayed enclosure at Hambledon. The detail (right) shows the flint arrowhead that killed him. It was only found when his bones were moved. Some of the bones of the infant found crushed beneath him can be seen, including its lower jaw (see also 14).*

dead, deliberately left exposed for the birds to pick clean. He has described the hilltop as a vast reeking cemetery, whose silence was broken only by the din of crows. This exposure of the dead is known as excarnation, and may have been a widely practised funerary rite in the causewayed enclosures. People probably also came here in large numbers to feast in memory of their dead. The remains of some 70 individuals were found during the archaeological excavations. Since this was about one fifth of the total volume of deposits, we can assume that the remains of up to 350 people had been deposited in the ditch fills. Presumably the remains of many more were laid out in the interior, but these have not survived.

Although the upper surfaces of the site have eroded considerably in the last 5000 years, the archaeologists were able to find the bottoms of pits which had been dug inside the large enclosure. Among the objects recovered from these were complete axes. These had not been discarded so much as deliberately placed. Why had the people of Hambledon buried these obviously useful tools?

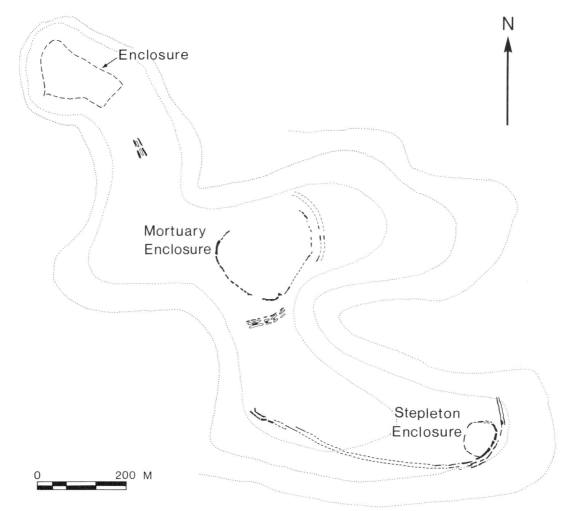

14 (Above) A plan of the causewayed enclosure complex on Hambledon Hill. The young man and baby were lying in the ditch of the Stepleton enclosure.

15 (Below) Knap Hill, a well-preserved causewayed enclosure. After a light snowfall the ditches, where the snow has melted, stand out clearly.

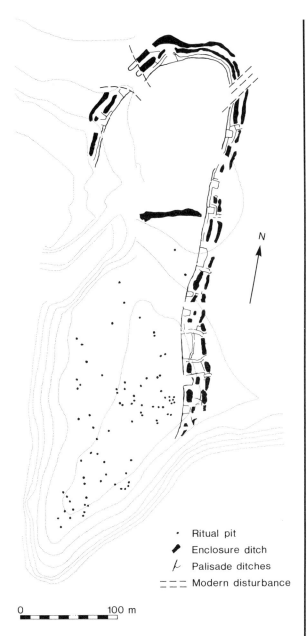

Ritual pit
Enclosure ditch
Palisade ditches
Modern disturbance

0   100 m

16 *The causewayed enclosure at Sarup in Denmark. As well as having ditches, this enclosure was surrounded by a complicated series of wooden palisades, visible as narrow post-trenches.*

3 ENCLOSURES

A characteristic of many prehistoric sites between the Neolithic and the Iron Age is that they were surrounded or enclosed by ditches and banks. Archaeologists call these ditched sites enclosures or enclosed settlements. The term is used in a very different sense from the land enclosures of the eighteenth and nineteenth centuries, when large tracts of common land were 'enclosed' and sold.

There is a considerable variety of Neolithic enclosures, few of which are thought to have been defensive or even used as permanent settlements. The causewayed enclosures (**17**) are so called because of the causeways left between sections of ditch. In other words the ditch was interrupted at regular intervals around its circuit by gaps. The mortuary enclosures were generally rectangular or oval and seem in plan very similar to long barrows but without the mound. Their name derives from finds of human bones in the ditch fills. Cursuses are even longer and wider than mortuary enclosures and may run for many miles. They do not seem to have enclosed settlements, though post-holes for a circular house were found at one end of the Springfield cursus in Essex. Henge monuments have their banks raised outside the ditch, as if to keep something in rather than out. Many of them have remains of large post-built circular structures inside them, though the precise purpose of these, whether roofed and permanently inhabited or not, is uncertain.

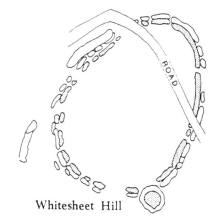

Whitesheet Hill

17 *The causewayed enclosure at Whitesheet Hill, showing the likely line of the earth bank.*

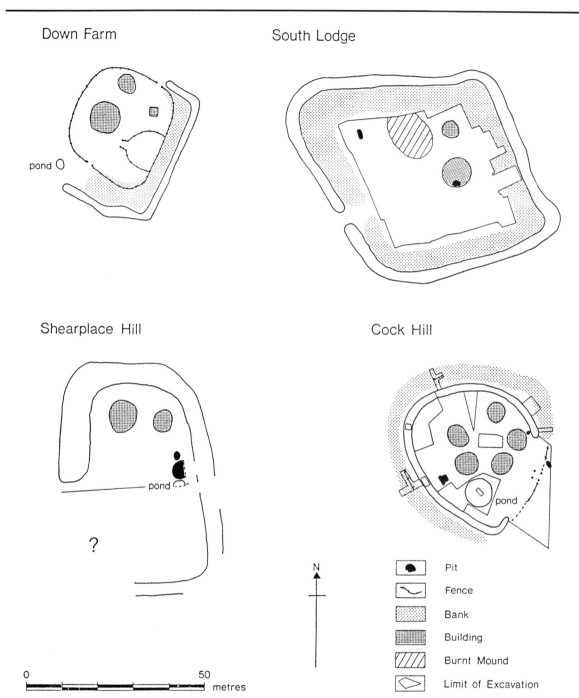

18 (Above) Later Bronze Age settlement
enclosures in southern Britain. (Right) Down
Farm in more detail.

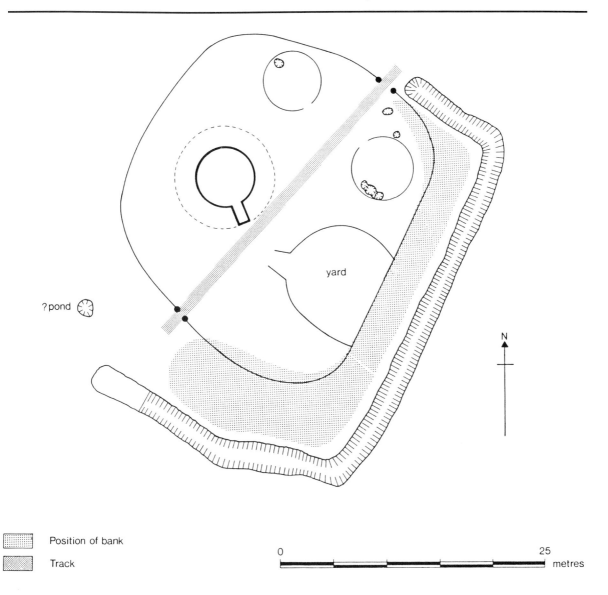

?pond

yard

N

■ Position of bank

▓ Track

0   25
                                                    metres

At the end of the Neolithic and in the Early Bronze Age, a number of large palisaded enclosures were constructed, some of them inside the henges, such as at Mount Pleasant at Dorchester. These enclosures were constructed from large timbers and may have had a defensive or military purpose.

It was not until the Later Bronze Age that enclosure ditches surrounded what we can claim as settlements. Groups of houses at South Lodge and Down Farm (**18**), on Cran-

borne Chase, were enclosed by partial or total ditch circuits. From 900 BC we find a series of very regular enclosures with buildings inside them, from Mucking in Essex (see **114**) to Navan in Ireland (see **115**). They may have been high status settlements but their precise geometrical forms suggest ceremonial use. The circular ditch at Navan enclosed a wooden palisade which may have served as an arena of some sort.

The axe: a symbol and a tool

The axes of these early farmers were made either of flint or of hard igneous rock (which is of volcanic origin). They were chipped into shape and then most of the igneous stone axes and some of the flint ones were laboriously ground and polished to provide a smooth surface. The axes of the gatherer-hunters were never polished, with the exception of polished axes from the Lough Neagh area (in northern Ireland). The stone axe was hafted in a carefully shaped axe handle of wood; complete examples have been found at Maguire's Bridge in Co. Fermanagh and at Etton causewayed enclosure in the Fens near Peterborough. In Brittany, carvings of axes, hafted and unhafted, were etched on to the sides of stone monuments. There is a good example at Gavrinis (**19**). This evidence from across the Channel supports our increasing awareness that stone axes had a significance beyond that of simple tools. Axes have been found throughout much of the British Isles, indicating that these farmers were clearing and managing woodland over all but the heaviest soils. In many cases the axeheads have broken or show evidence of continuous resharpening. But there are significant numbers which had never been used to cut down trees. They were deposited in what were no doubt special places, seemingly without thought of recovery. Some axes were clearly never intended for use in chopping wood. Many axes, including the beautiful, thin and finely polished axes of jadeite show no signs of wear on their blades and many would have shattered if they had ever been used. There are over 70 green jadeite axes found in Britain but made in the Alps. As we have seen, one of these was placed under a piece of wood next to the Sweet Track; other items such as a small bag of flint blades and a group of pots containing food had also been deposited by the trackway. Were these casually lost or left there, perhaps as offerings? Was the trackway constructed for purposes as much spiritual as practical?

Analysis of the mineral composition of stone axes made from igneous rocks shows that they were produced from a wide variety of sources. More than two thirds of them cannot be linked to any particular source of stone but the remainder can be matched with specific outcrops of rock. In some cases the very sites where the axes were made can be identified, revealed by the debris of chipped stone. One of

19 *A broken menhir showing the icons of the farming package: a ?plough; a cow; a sheep; a ?crook/corn ear/sickle; and a hafted axe. This piece of the menhir was incorporated into a chambered tomb at Gavrinis, Brittany. The other two pieces were built into two tombs 8 km (5 miles) away.*

20 *Pike o' Stickle in Langdale, where stone was quarried to make axes in the Neolithic.*

these, near Carmarthen (Dyfed), was not an outcrop but a group of glacial erratics, stones which had been transported from the Preseli Mountains by an Ice Age glacier. Other axe-making sites were located at the rock outcrops themselves. The most productive of these were located off Land's End (now underwater due to post-glacial sea level changes), at Graig Llydd

in North Wales and on Pike o'Stickle in Langdale in the Lake District (**20**). One of the largest of these production sites or 'factories' was in Langdale, where production had begun by *c*.3700 BC. A huge area of 20 ha (49 acres) of fairly inaccessible mountain was devoted to quarrying stone and chipping axe roughouts, which were then taken off the mountain to be polished. Some of the quarrying was carried out on a near vertical face perched above the valley. The quality of stone is no better here than in other parts of the quarry but people were obviously drawn to this most dangerous and inaccessible place to quarry stone for axes. Many of the more accessible areas on the outcrop had not been quarried, even though the quality of stone was just as good. Not only were people extracting stone for axes from the more dangerous spots on the mountain, but they were neither systematic nor efficient in their task. The axe quarry workers were not specialists. It is probable that the work of quarrying and shaping was carried out on a seasonal basis, during the slack times of the farming year, perhaps when the sheep were led to the high pastures. The production site was shared between at least two groups, since pounding stones of two different materials were brought by the axe makers from two different locations below the mountain and left in the quarries.

The igneous stone axe factories are all located in western and northern Britain (with two in northern Ireland at Tievebulliagh and Rathlin Island) (**21**), areas which previously supported sizeable populations of gatherer-hunters. Perhaps it was their descendants who initiated the axe making in order to exchange them for gifts from the farmers. Flint occurs in the chalk strata which outcrop in southern and eastern Britain. Flint axes were certainly being produced from *c*.4000 BC in Sussex from at least four flint mines: at Church Hill (Findon), Harrow Hill, Blackpatch and Longdown. These consisted of groups of shafts dug deep into the chalk to extract the unweathered seams of flint. There are other flint mines in southern Britain which probably date to this period, including the earliest phases at Grimes Graves in Norfolk (though this mining complex did not really develop until much later) (**colour plates 4 and 5**). Unlike the igneous stone axes, flint from different sources is difficult to characterize so archaeologists have had only minor success in plotting its distribution from source. No doubt the vast majority of flint tools, and many of the axes, came from surface deposits of flint. Why did they bother to dig deep shafts for it on top of high chalk hills? The deeper layers of flint were less affected by frost-shattering and were better raw materials for large tools such as axes; but the mines still need not have been located on exposed hilltops.

Another curious feature of the location of many of these early axe factories is their marginal situation within Britain, not far from the coast. In addition, their locations are often

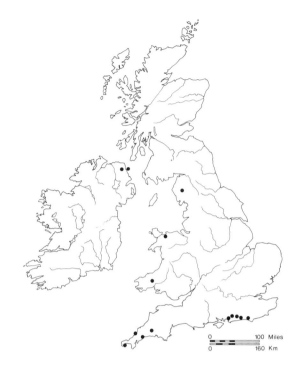

21 *The distribution of Early Neolithic axe quarries and mines.*

spectacular, sited on sea cliffs or high up in the hills and mountains. This is no doubt explained in part by the available outcropping of suitable rocks and by the lack of tree cover in these locations. But these places may have had a greater spiritual significance for the manufacturers, perched between the land, the sea and the heavens. The steep rock face at Pike o'Stickle is not a sensible location to quarry stone for axes. Perhaps the axes that were made here had a more powerful magical significance than others. Perhaps there was something special about these places where the land ran out, on the edges of existence. For us, mining and quarrying are practical activities, guided by efficiency and expediency. Neolithic quarrying was carried out under very different logical premises, where the rocks themselves may have been considered to have spiritual properties.

The axes produced at these sources have been recovered from all over the British Isles (**22**). The crude blanks, or 'roughouts', were carried down the mountain to the margins of the lowlands, where they were ground and

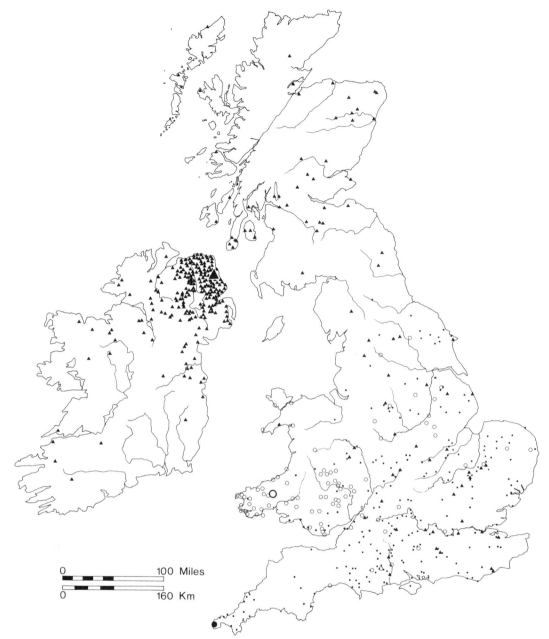

22 *Map showing the distribution of axes made at Tievebulliagh and Rathlin Island in Co. Antrim; the distribution of axes made in west Wales; and the distribution of axes made at Land's End in Cornwall.*

Source and distribution of axes from:

▲ ▴ Northern Ireland

○ ○ Wales

● • Cornwall

polished. The finished products were then transported far and wide. Axes from Langdale have turned up in east Yorkshire in large numbers and axes from Cornwall are frequent finds in East Anglia. Tievebulliagh axes are largely found within 40 km (25 miles) of their source but have been found in Shetland as well as southern Britain. How did these objects travel so far? It has been suggested that the raw material may have been initially transported by glaciers as unmodified rocks, and that these glacial erratics were later fashioned into axes. This was no doubt so in some cases but we now know, from the existence of axe factories, that they were carried away from their sources by people. It has been suggested that they were exchanged individually from one person to the next, a multitude of short distance exchanges resulting in an overall movement of hundreds of kilometres. Or many may have been transported in bulk, perhaps by boat along the coast. The reality, over nearly a thousand years, was probably far more complicated, involving individual exchanges and bulk transactions. It was probably very different to our modern notions of trade involving markets, buying and selling. The trade in axes was no doubt only one of the few material manifestations of long distance contacts. People needed to keep in touch over wide areas and promote alliances between different groups. We may guess that they used these networks to find marriage partners, to exchange gifts and other goods and to develop groups of trading partners. The small and often scattered communities also needed places where they could come together in large numbers at particular times to celebrate, to worship and to exchange news and gifts. At these events their beliefs about the world around them and the role of human beings within the cosmos would be celebrated and reaffirmed in their rituals. We must not forget that simple technologies are often used in societies which are highly sophisticated and have very complex beliefs and rituals. The simple material life of these early farmers seems to mask a far from primitive spiritual existence.

Causewayed enclosures have produced more than their fair share of axes. As well as the remains of human skeletons, they sometimes have dense deposits of refuse. From the animal bones and pottery, archaeologists have deduced that these are the remains of feasts. Perhaps people came here from miles around to celebrate and to exchange goods such as axes (**23**). There are problems with these rubbish deposits; why discard this excellent fertilizer when it could be spread on the fields? Were these enclosures in fact shrines to fertility? Was this 'symbolic manure'? All of the enclosures excavated in any detail have produced human bones, normally from the ditch fills. At Etton, the interior of the enclosure was divided into two halves; one half was full of deposits of cremated bone, both animal and human. Perhaps these places were associated with ensuring the continued fertility of the land as well as the people. From death came rebirth.

The causewayed enclosures are some of the largest monuments of the earlier Neolithic. Digging the ditch of the outer ring (of three ditches) at Windmill Hill (Wiltshire) would have required the equivalent of 48,000 hours of labour in our terms – or 100 people working for several months. In the 1970s archaeologists regarded them as 'central places', territorial centres at which people congregated. Recent study of their local environments (from snails and insects) indicates that the enclosures at Windmill Hill, Knap Hill, Maiden Castle and the enclosures on the Sussex Downs were surrounded by woodland, on the margins of the cleared land. Perhaps they really were sacred places in the wilderness, where the fertility of the natural world could be tapped and harnessed to ensure the successful reproduction of crops, animals and people.

The landscape of the early farmers
It took the earliest farmers many hundreds of years to make much of a dent in the forest cover. Clearances at Ballyscullion, Ballynagilly, Beaghmore and the Somerset Levels regenerated to forest after a few hundred years or even less. Such clearances were relatively small (c.35–80 sq. km (14–31 sq. miles)). While stone axes are relatively effective at chopping down trees when used by experienced hands, much of the clearance was probably achieved by ring-barking and burning the trees. Many sites have produced tree throw-holes which indicate that trees were burned at their bases, presumably to kill and weaken them, before being blown over by the wind or even pulled down by farmers. There is some controversy over the extent to which this 'slash and burn' clearance (known as 'landnam' from the

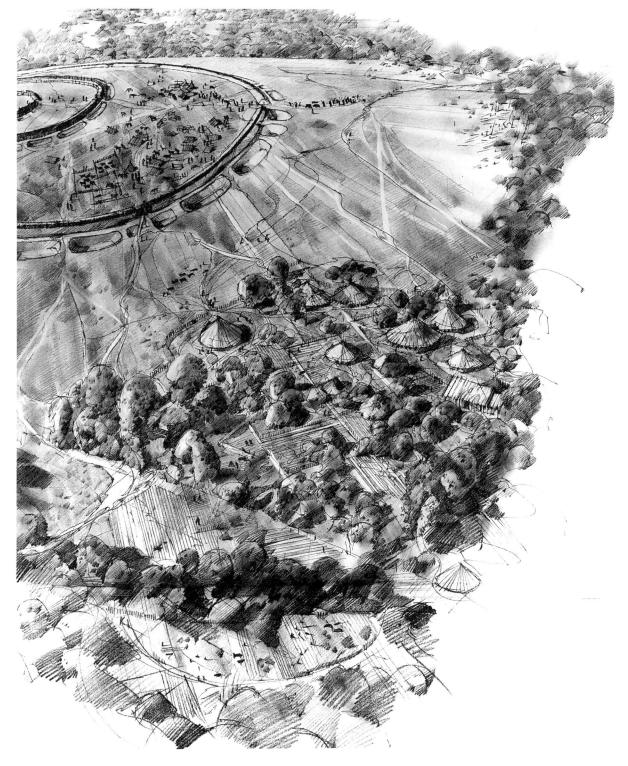

23 *Reconstruction of a ceremony at a
causewayed enclosure.*

Danish word) affected soil fertility. The layer of wood ash provided nutrients for the crops sown in that soil. After a few years the plot might be abandoned because the nutrients were largely exhausted. The farmers then moved on to the next section of woodland to be felled. However, modern experiments have shown that moderate yields of wheat and barley are sustainable without manuring or fertilizers for at least 50–100 years. The experiments are still going on so we do not know just how long these yields can be obtained. Much depends on the type of soil. Some areas, once cleared, never really recovered, such as the sandy Breckland after 4000 BC, or the area around Goodland (Co. Antrim), where clearance and cultivation led to the formation of heath and peat after 3300 BC.

In the centuries after 4000 BC, the time of the elm decline, considerable inroads were being made into the forest. In many places, the valleys and uplands were being opened up in a series of large clearings. These were edged by dense tangles of thorn, brush and saplings, while the cleared area went through a process of regeneration as cultivated land became pasture and then hazel coppice, before returning to woodland. Cultivation was achieved by a simple form of plough, the ard, as well as by spade digging. At South Street, Avebury, a rip-ard (a more robust ard with a deeper digging point) was used to prepare ground for cultivation. It went so deep that it scored furrows into the chalk bedrock. This was no light piece of equipment but a heavy implement which tore a deep furrow in the ground, no doubt pulled by an ox team. Otherwise ard cultivation was relatively shallow, scoring the ground surface in two opposing directions to create a lattice of disturbed ground that could then be planted. Archaeologists disagree whether these communities were settled farmers practising intensive agricultural methods or were shifting cultivators using more extensive methods. Were they similar to farmers of several hundred years ago before the agricultural revolution, intensively ploughing the land and efficiently raising herds of animals within each farm, or were they reliant on a variety of cultivation methods and food sources, including wild resources, which they harvested across a wide area? We know from the few occupation sites preserved that they consumed large numbers of hazelnuts and other wild plant foods. We also know that they were being very selective in the ways that they

culled their cattle, as we shall see later.

One of the most extraordinary finds from Hambledon Hill was only 5 mm (¼ in) long. It was a carbonized grape pip, accidentally preserved by fire. We often find carbonized grain because the drying and roasting processes used to prepare the seeds for storage or grinding were likely to cause some of the seeds to be burned. The chances of finding a burnt grape pip, however, are considerably less than finding a burnt seed of grain. This could have been a rare and exotic import from overseas, perhaps dried fruit. But equally, the people of Wessex may have been growing their own grapes. The climate was slightly warmer than today so this suggestion is perhaps not that surprising.

The grape pip, like the jadeite axes, indicates long distance contacts across the Channel. Another indication of the sophistication of these people is their concern with building and construction. In Co. Mayo, Ireland, field walls have been found buried beneath the peat at Behy and Glenulra (24) and at Belderg Beg, where they have been dated to c.3300–3000 BC. At Carn Brea in Cornwall, a defended enclosure of similar date was built next to small field plots cleared of stones. These stones had been heaped into small piles, known as clearance cairns. These are some of the earliest fields in the British Isles. The most prominent and widespread landmarks of the early farmers were their monumental tombs, built of earth, stone or timber. These, the fields, the mines and quarries, the enclosures and the large clearances indicate that the farmers were intent on stamping their mark on the land, in contrast to the gatherer-hunters who, it seems, lived less intrusively in their environment. To what extent farming was brought by immigrants or adopted by groups of gatherer-hunters is not known; presumably both immigrants and indigenous communities were involved in its development in the British Isles.

The tombs of the ancestors
The coastal fringes of western Europe, from Spain to Sweden, are dotted with the remains of large, collective monuments for the dead built by the early farmers. Some are round, others rectangular and yet others trapezoidal or irregular. They are not found in inland Europe, where the longhouse farmers buried their dead individually in simple earth graves. Indeed, their coastal distribution, the 'Atlantic

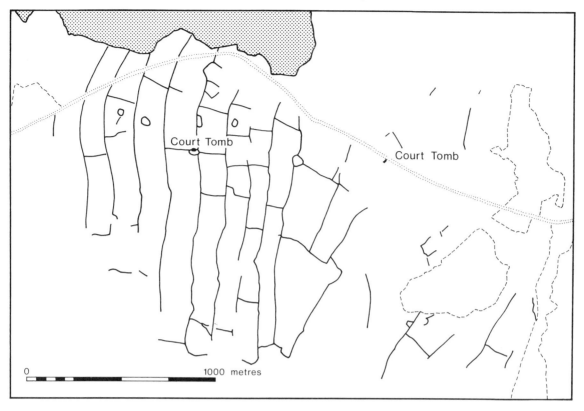

24 *The Neolithic stone walls and fields at Behy and Glenulra, Ireland.*

facade' as it has been called, corresponds to the regions where high densities of gatherer-hunters had previously lived. Was this coincidence or was the building of these tombs somehow caused by the meeting of these two distinctive lifestyles? It has been suggested that the builders of these tombs were marking their territories. As farmers came to the edge of the continent into areas populated by gatherer-hunters, there was increasing competition for the land's resources. They set up markers which would stand for ever to represent the permanent link between a community, its ancestral dead and the land which they farmed. These were not simply places to dispose of the dead but monuments where the ancestors resided, giving their sanction to the use of that land by their descendants (**25**).

The earliest dates for tombs come from Brittany, where the oldest ones may be nearly 7000 years old. One tomb in the British Isles, at Carrowmore in Ireland, has produced a radiocarbon date of the same age but there is controversy about its reliability. If the Carrowmore date is an error (which is likely), then tombs in the British Isles were built much later, within the period of 4000–3200 BC. They may have been built over a period of little more than five hundred years, a relatively short-lived fashion in archaeological terms! Even in the areas where they are densest they need only have been built at a rate of one every 20–30 years within a period of 800 to 1000 years. The average labour expended on a small tomb is about 10,000 person hours; a small group of 20 people could have built one within a few months after the harvest.

The distribution of surviving tombs in the different regions of the British Isles is uneven in a way that cannot simply be explained by their destruction in some areas over the last 6000 years. The south of Ireland has very few tombs of this period, yet the presence of other finds in the region, including foundations for a wooden house at Tankardstown, indicate that people were living here. Perhaps some areas

41

25 *Reconstruction of a funerary ceremony outside a chambered long barrow.*

were regarded as ancestral homelands and others were not. Perhaps the tombs were placed in areas with competing land claims. There is some evidence that tombs are more common in areas of secondary settlement, away from the areas of earliest occupation.

The shapes of the tombs must also be explained. It is over 30 years ago that someone noticed the similarities of the round tombs to gatherer-hunters' houses and the rectangular or trapezoidal tombs to the longhouses of central Europe. The tombs were probably modelled on house styles, not necessarily those of the

immediate vicinity, to provide houses for the ancestors (**26**). It is curious that they were built so much more solidly than the small and flimsy wooden houses of the living. They embodied a permanence of the ancestral lineages, in contrast to the fleeting and transitory nature of individual lives. The community was far more important than any individuals within it. Tombs were more than places to dispose of the dead. They were shrines to the ancestors who may well have been considered 'supernatural' beings. In many societies around the world, the ancestors have been considered to affect the well-being of the living. The ancestors may ward off evil, ensure the fertility of crops and herds and protect the community. Feasts are held in their honour while offerings and sacrifices are made to them in return for their

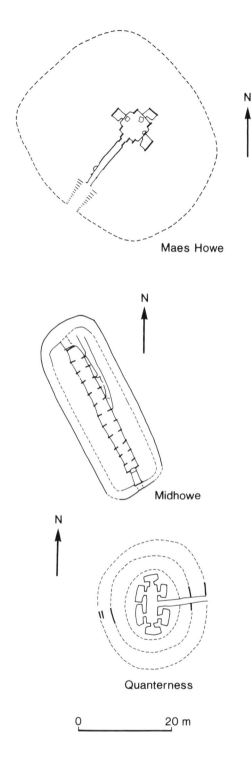

N

N

N

0   20 m

26 *Plans of the various types of Orcadian Neolithic tomb, showing the stalled type (Midhowe) and two examples of the cellular type (Maes Howe and Quanterness).*

Maes Howe

Midhowe

Quanterness

intervention. Many archaeologists consider that the concern shown by Neolithic people for their dead can be interpreted as a similar belief in the power of ancestors.

The styles of tombs varied from region to region. The chalklands and lowlands of southern and eastern Britain are characterized by long mounds, often piled up on wooden structures. The tombs of the Cotswolds were faced with drystone masonry using the local limestone. They often included internal stone-built chambers which seem to have been used for centuries. One of these large chambers, within a very long mound at West Kennet (**colour plate 2**), incorporated drystone masonry of limestone which must have come from many miles away in the Cotswolds. There is disagreement whether these stones were carried by the tomb-builders or dragged to the area by glaciers in the previous glaciation.

In the western regions of the British Isles there are a number of tombs constructed with upright stones and capstones, like giant stone tables held up on vertical slabs. These are known as portal dolmens or cromlechs. Some of them are thought to have been covered by earth mounds or stone cairns. Pentre Ifan, in the Preseli Mountains, is a fine example (**28**). In Ireland is a group known as court cairns, the front of the tomb enclosing a semi-circular courtyard or forecourt. The most spectacular tombs of this period are the passage graves of Ireland and the very north of Scotland, especially the islands of Orkney. Those from the Bend in the Boyne and Orkney are impressive feats of engineering. They were huge structures, up to 95 m (312 ft) in diameter and 12 m (39 ft) high, with revetted stone walls. A long passage, formed of enormous stone slabs, led to a chamber roofed with stones by a technique known as corbelling: each stone protruded inwards a little further than the one underneath to form a dome.

Some tombs started off as wooden chambers, later covered by soil or stones to form a mound or cairn. At Street House long barrow, in Cleveland (see **116**), a timber structure was erected and then burned down before the mound was constructed. Others appear to have been built in a single episode. Some were built initially as circular tombs which were then remodelled into rectangular forms. There was an enormous range of variations in tomb construction. A recent find from Fengate, near Peterborough,

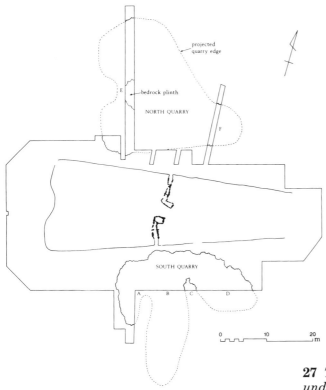

27 *The long cairn at Hazleton (Gloucestershire) under excavation and a plan of the excavation, showing the burial chambers.*

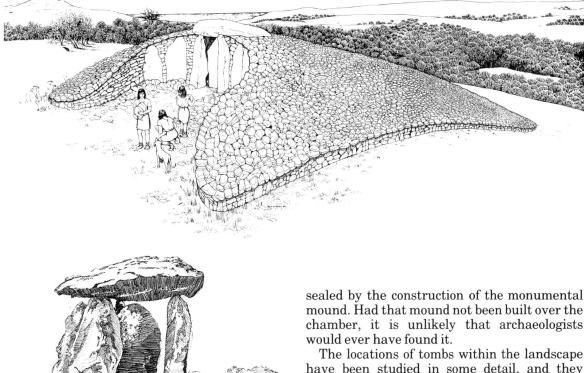

28 *Reconstruction and drawing of Pentre Ifan, a portal dolmen in the Preseli mountains.*

illustrates the archaeologists' difficulties in finding some of these tombs. During excavations of a much later settlement archaeologists uncovered a large pit containing the partly disarticulated remains of several individuals from this period. Had a mound ever been built over the pit then it might have been recognized as a long barrow by the archaeologists. How many more hidden graves like this are waiting to be found? Nearby in the Cambridgeshire Fens at Haddenham, a recently discovered long barrow, buried until the recent rapid shrinkage of the peat, hid the wooden remains of a sunken burial chamber (**29**). Enormous timbers had been employed in the construction yet they had been trimmed to form a low container covered by loose, roughly hewn planks. Inside were five articulated corpses. This wooden chamber would not have been visible from any distance, even in the flat landscape of the Fens. Some time had elapsed before the chamber had been

sealed by the construction of the monumental mound. Had that mound not been built over the chamber, it is unlikely that archaeologists would ever have found it.

The locations of tombs within the landscape have been studied in some detail, and they seem to have varied from region to region. In Orkney the smaller, probably earlier, tombs were located on the margins of the lighter soils often at highly visible points in the landscape, by the sea or up on a hillside. In the uplands of southern and eastern England chambered tombs and long barrows were often located at the heads of valleys, presumably placed above the valley settlements (**30**). Along the scarp slope of the Cotswolds, in Gloucestershire, chambered tombs like Hetty Pegler's Tump and Nympsfield occupy prominent positions overlooking the Severn valley to the north, though their associated communities were probably to the south, in the valleys of the dip slope. In the Midlands tombs were often in low-lying positions, in the wide river valleys rather than on the hillslopes. A detailed study of tombs of Co. Leitrim has shown that all but one were located on or adjacent to the restricted areas of fertile, well-drained soils surrounded by heavy claylands. They seem to have been prominent features of the social landscape, often in close proximity to the dwellings of the living. Study of the soils from underneath tombs indicates that some were built on land which had been ploughed, like South Street in Avebury. The vast majority were sited on land

29 *The wooden plank chamber under the long barrow at Haddenham. It had contained five human skeletons.*

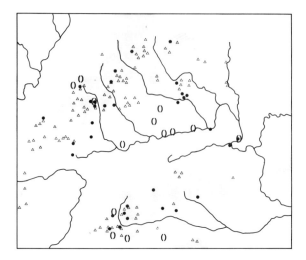

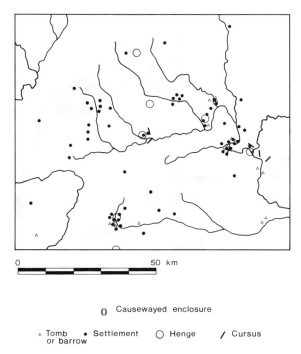

0   Causewayed enclosure

△ Tomb   • Settlement   ○ Henge   / Cursus
or barrow

30 *The distribution of Early and Late Neolithic tombs and settlements in the Upper Thames.*

which was used for pasture. It seems that tombs were placed not in the wild and uncultivated areas well away from the settlements, but close to the farmland of the living.

We call these monuments tombs because they often contain human skeletons, sometimes complete but most often disarticulated. Perhaps their role as repositories of human remains was only one of several; we would not consider a parish church to be simply a tomb. Although many of the stone chambered tombs could have been entered and filled with bodies and bones over many centuries, very few tombs seem to have been filled to bursting. Calculations of living populations from numbers of individuals in tombs would indicate a population of less than 250 at any one time in southern Britain! This is excessively small and archaeologists consider that only a small proportion of the population was placed in them. Who was buried in them? While we wait to see whether DNA analysis of the bones will tell us whether the occupants of a tomb were closely related genetically, we can only speculate. Were the individuals whose remains were placed in a tomb members of a ruling family or lineage? Or were there different lineages roughly equal in status, with each tomb including a selection of bodies and bones of ancestral members of the lineage?

There are hints that bodies were left to rot either somewhere outside the tombs or in them, before the bones were rearranged. The bones from Wayland's Smithy (Oxfordshire) had probably been gnawed by rodents prior to burial. Some of these and bones in a barrow at Skendleby (Lincolnshire), had snails' eggs on them. Since this particular species of snail lived only above ground, the bones must have been

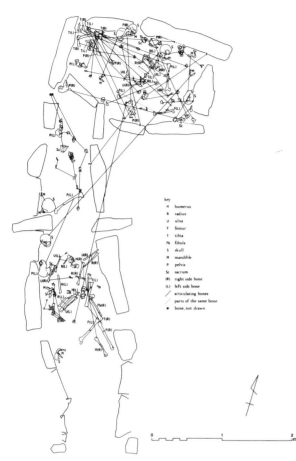

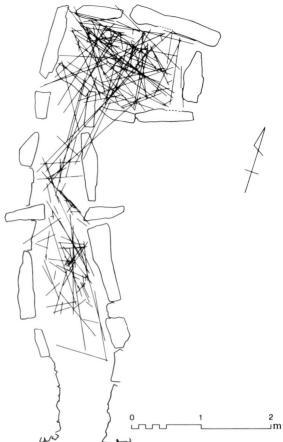

key

H	humerus
R	radius
U	ulna
F	femur
T	tibia
Fb	fibula
S	skull
M	mandible
P	pelvis
Sc	sacrum
(R)	right side bone
(L)	left side bone
/	articulating bones
/	parts of the same bone
●	bone, not drawn

31 *Bones in the south chamber of Hazleton long cairn. (Left) Articulating bones; (right) paired bones. The joins show how the skeletons have been disarticulated.*

left for some time in an accessible and open place. There is a strong possibility that the bones from the Ascott-under-Wychwood barrow (Oxfordshire) were excarnated. It was hoped that careful excavation at the tomb of Hazleton (Gloucestershire) would clarify whether the bodies had been placed in the stone chambers and then left to rot, or had rotted before the bones were placed in the tomb (**31**, **32** and see **27**). Unfortunately the results of painstaking refitting of the bones and plotting of their findspots could not fully solve this problem. However, one of the chambers had become closed off during the tomb's use, when its entrance collapsed. The bodies in this sealed chamber had been sat up against the walls of the passage and chamber and had fallen into heaps of bones. In the other chamber, the bones had been sorted to some degree with skulls

grouped in one area and long bones in another. A final articulated burial of a man holding a flint core (from which to knap tools) was placed in its entrance.

Other tombs indicate some degree of sorting bones. The layout of human bones in the tombs is perhaps clearest where the bodies were placed in separate chambers. In a number of chambered tombs such as West Kennet, the innermost chamber held the remains of predominantly adult men. Other chambers contained bones mainly of women and children. Placing of the dead in these tombs seems to have been organized along the lines of age and gender. There are interesting comparisons with the causewayed enclosures: it is principally adults that are found in tombs while enclosures have the remains of many more children than adults. Also, skulls are common in the enclosures but are generally under-represented in the bones in tombs. The rubbish from causewayed enclosures includes a preponderance of cattle bones. Cattle bones were also placed in the tombs of the Cotswolds and Severn Valley,

32 *The south chamber at Hazleton, filled with disarticulated human bones.*

together with the remains of the ancestors, while pig bones, possibly the remains of feasting, predominated in the deposits outside. The cattle bones from Hambledon Hill are primarily those of older females and young calves. One archaeologist has interpreted these as the kill residue from a dairying herd kept in the settlement enclosure at Hambledon Hill. Others consider that the enclosure was ceremonial in purpose and that calves and cows were selected from many herds in the region and brought to the enclosure to be killed and eaten in the ceremonies.

Some of the later tombs, after *c*.3500 BC, were rather different. In Yorkshire a new style of burial seems to have begun around 3000 BC, involving a burial rite which was still collective but with the individual skeletons left intact. Previously in this region the early farmers' monumental tombs were long barrows with collections of disarticulated human bones, but they included a number of unusual elements. Some tomb facades and chambers were deliber-

ately burned, with individual corpses cremated. Their remains consisted of small piles of tiny fragments of burnt bone. Where the bodies were not burnt, their skeletons were normally disarticulated and incomplete, as in other regions, but some were buried complete. The new burial rite involved the placing of crouched burials (bodies laid flat but with the knees brought up to the chin in a foetal position), sometimes in large numbers, in a large pit and with an enormous mound built over the top. The best known of these is Duggleby Howe where two shafts were cut into the chalk (**33**). In the larger of the two, what seems to have been a wooden chamber was constructed at the bottom. Inside was the corpse of an adult man with a pottery bowl and a handful of flints. Also in the pit was another corpse and a human skull. In the other pit were two bodies, one with a beautifully shaped and polished flint knife and the other with arrowheads and other flints, a bone pin, the tusks of wild boar and teeth of beaver, thought to have been used as tools. Within the rest of the mound were another ten bodies, of children as well as adults. One adult was equipped with a very fine flint adze (like an axe but with a horizontal rather than vertical

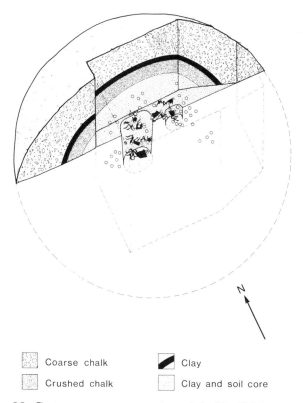

Probably some five hundred years later, another layer of mound material was added and another 43 cremations were put in. This layer was capped by a thick sealing layer of clay. Finally, a huge heap of chalk rubble was piled on top. From aerial photography, we know that this enormous mound lies at the centre of a huge circle or horseshoe, formed by a causewayed ditch and enclosing an area of over 10 ha (25 acres) (see **119**).

These burials of articulated corpses are known from other parts of the British Isles at this time. One has been excavated at Barrow Hills (Oxfordshire) (see **85**). At the centre of a ploughed out oval mound was a grave with two articulated skeletons, laid out in a crouched position. One was a man, equipped only with a small belt toggle, while the other was a woman, with a polished flint blade. One of the two ditches enclosing the burial mound was filled with deposits that had been deliberately put there: broken pots, flints, antlers and human skulls. A similar group of burials, found in tombs in Ireland, is known as the Linkardstown group. The Yorkshire burials have the most varied and beautiful sets of grave goods. Were they chiefs and their families? Or were they ordinary individuals honoured by the community for other reasons? Similar flint axes and knives have been found on settlement sites, but they are rough and poorly made in comparison to the beautifully crafted items found in the graves.

| Coarse chalk | Clay |
| Crushed chalk | Clay and soil core |

33 *Cut-away reconstruction of the Neolithic burial mound at Duggleby Howe, Yorkshire.*

blade), a macehead made out of antler (the top of an ornamental staff) and an arrowhead. There were also ten cremations in this mound.

4 SKELETONS AND BURIAL

We rarely see dead bodies, skeletons or even human bones. Yet they were common sights to people of the Neolithic and Bronze Age. Some of the causewayed enclosures were open-air cemeteries where bodies were left on the ground to decompose. Bodies were also placed in tombs, either complete or after they had rotted, when bundles of bones might be collected together and put in the tomb.

We do not know what was done with the dead in the Mesolithic. Groups of burials are known from other parts of Europe but not in Britain. Perhaps corpses were left on the ground or placed in trees. In the Earlier Neolithic bodies were certainly left to rot and fall apart, a process known as excarnation (natural defleshing of the bones). These disarticulated bones were scattered or even positioned in the ditches and interiors of causewayed enclosures or inside the chambers (of wood or of stone) of long barrows. By the Later Neolithic people were burying bodies intact. The bones of their skeletons remained articulated, so that when we excavate them we find whole skeletons rather than groups of disarticulated bones.

The burial of whole corpses continued into the Earlier Bronze Age, with individuals being interred under round mounds. Sometimes the corpse was buried in a pit but in other cases, such as at Bush Barrow, the body was laid on bare chalk after the turf and topsoil had been scraped away. Generally bodies were buried in crouched or flexed positions (in the foetal position or with the legs bent) as at West Cotton (**34** and see also **72**). Only rarely, as at Bush Barrow, were they buried on their backs with their legs extended, as we do today. In many

34 *The crouched skeleton of a man buried under a mound at West Cotton (Northamptonshire). The grave goods, including a beaker, now squashed, were placed by his feet. At the extreme right is a flint dagger (see 72).*

cases the mounds were dug into, either to place secondary burials in the mound or for other reasons that we do not fully understand. These shallow pits were not to rob bones or grave goods but may have been dug as part of a ceremony for communicating with the dead.

Archaeologists from Verulamium Museum recently found a logboat burial at Old Park-bury, near St Albans. A decomposed and dis-articulated corpse had been placed in the hollowed-out boat, along with a wooden box

and another wooden container. Body and boat were then set alight, not too successfully. With a radiocarbon date of around 4700 BC, this may be the earliest cremation in Britain. Whether it was performed by gatherer-hunters, we do not know. Cremation was rare in the Earlier Neo-lithic but is known in Yorkshire and Ireland in that period, It was more common in the Later Neolithic and Earlier Bronze Age. In the Middle Bronze Age cremation became the preva-lent rite. Cemeteries with large numbers of cremations, often in urns, are known from all over the British Isles. In the Late Bronze Age it seems that a certain proportion of the popula-tion were dumped in rivers. It is likely that most people at that time were cremated with their ashes scattered or buried in shallow pits without any pots.

Houses and settlements

The houses of the early farmers are rarely found, but it seems they lived principally in rectangular ones. Houses were normally built of timber and were small, insubstantial and impermanent in contrast to the tombs. Some have been found under or adjacent to tombs, as at Ballyglass in Ireland. Others have been

located by chance. The earliest was found at Ballynagilly and is about 6000 years old (**35**). Houses are also known from Scotland (Bal-bridie) and Wales (Gwernvale). The remains of the wooden structure at Balbridie, dating to about 3700 BC, indicate that it was more of a hall than a house. At 13 m (43 ft) wide and 26 m (85 ft) long it is easily the largest known

35 *Reconstruction of the earliest Neolithic house in the British Isles, at Ballynagilly.*

Early Neolithic house in the British Isles. Perhaps it was more than just a dwelling.

In a number of houses the entrances appear to have been in the centre of the end walls but a more common feature is that the entrance was in one corner of the house. At Fengate the foundations of a wooden house shared the same NNW–SSE alignment as a much larger rectangular ditched enclosure of unknown purpose some hundreds of metres away. Intriguingly, this enclosure also had a corner entrance. A few kilometres away, at Castor, two large enclosures with corner entrances have been recently examined. Corner entrances are also known in some of the funerary monuments of this date such as the sub-rectangular barrow at Barrow Hills. The houses seem to have had a central hearth and in some cases were divided across the hearth into two rooms. The walls were constructed of planks set vertically in bedding trenches and presumably the roofs were thatched.

Habitation areas of this period are hard to find since they have left little trace and have suffered from later agricultural practices. Occasionally, however, we find them well preserved. Under the tomb at Hazleton was an earlier occupation layer, but with no evidence of any structures. In the vicinity of two hearths was a spread of animal bones, flint waste, pottery and burnt seeds. At Lismore Fields, near Buxton (Derbyshire), three houses have been excavated. Two of them were so close together that they may have been joined, or were put up at different times. These were simple rectangular dwellings, built with wooden uprights. They were no larger than 5 × 8 m (16½ × 26 ft) in dimension and could have housed an extended family group in each.

Recent excavations in the Western Isles of Scotland have uncovered a small settlement built on an artificial island in Loch Olabhat (**36**). Artificial islands, known as crannogs, were built and used in Scotland until a few hundred years ago. They are formed out of heaps of stone which are constructed into platforms in estuaries and lakes. The crannog at Loch Olabhat seems to have been shaped like a round stone tomb, with bowed out front walls meeting at the entrance. A small rectangular house and other features were located on the crannog inside a timber palisade.

In the Hullbridge estuary in Essex, another settlement has been partially excavated. Originally on dry land, the site is now underwater as the result of sea level changes caused by slow readjustment of the European landmass after the retreat of the ice sheets. The settlement had been covered in silt and is now exposed at its ground level at low tide. Excavations when the tide was out, but still in exceptionally muddy and wet conditions, recovered a vast number of pottery sherds and grains of wheat, barley and other crops. There were lots of small gullies and depressions in the land surface but none of these seem to have formed the foundations for houses. Perhaps the area investigated was not large enough. Perhaps the houses were very flimsy, or maybe they were extremely irregular. It is on sites like this where the land surface is preserved that we stand the best chance of finding house remains, but it can be extremely difficult. The ideal situation is undoubtedly where the timbers have survived or where the houses were built of stone.

At Knap of Howar in Orkney two stone houses were built side by side, joined by a connecting door (**37**). They were built into a midden (a rubbish dump) which was so large that it may have provided effective insulation, in addition to the stone walls. Their inhabitants had cleared the islands of woodland by this period and, fortunately for us, were constructing their houses out of stone. Each house was divided into two or three rooms. In the larger, the innermost room was furnished with a central hearth, a pot set into a hole and a large grinding stone to prepare either porridge or bread. Grooves in the subsoil had probably held wooden planks, forming beds or seats. The outer room of the larger house was paved and furnished with a stone bench against the south

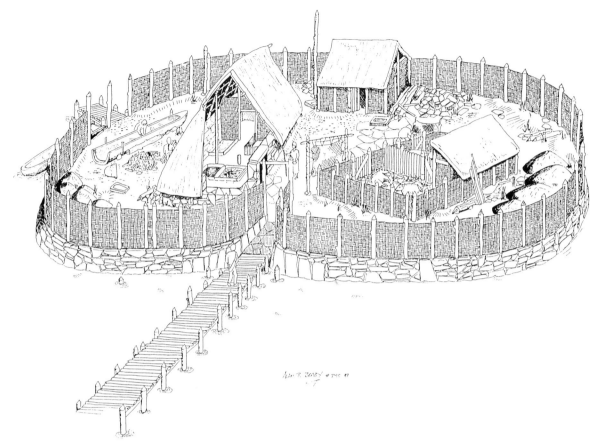

36 *Reconstruction of one phase of the Neolithic crannog settlement at Loch Olabhat in the Western Isles.*

wall that may have served as another bed. The smaller house had a tiny front room but its rear was divided into two areas, a central hearth area and an inner recess. This backroom was elaborately furnished with stone wall cupboards and recessed bays which may have been used to store food.

It is also from Orkney that we get another detailed and intimate picture of people's lives in the Neolithic. The chambered tombs at Quanterness and Isbister were surprisingly full of human bones, considerably more than the sparse, mixed and incomplete bone groups from other British tombs of the period. They provide a suitably large sample to give us details of people's physical features, their life expectancy and their general well-being. The interpretation of their features and health can be extended to the rest of the population in the

British Isles at that time, based on what we know from analysis of smaller numbers of skeletons elsewhere.

Women averaged 160 cm (5 ft 3 in) in height (between 147 cm (4 ft 10 in) and 163 cm (5 ft 4 in)) and men 170 cm (5 ft 7 in) (between 160 cm (5 ft 3 in) and 178 cm (5 ft 10 in)). They were thus only slightly smaller than ourselves, probably largely as the result of poor diet. The people of Isbister were more muscular than those in Quanterness, possibly because they were regular cliff-climbers; otherwise there were few differences between the two populations. Teeth were often worn down but were generally in very good condition, in contrast to our own. The few cases of caries or abcesses in the mouth were, however, very nasty and a few individuals must have suffered considerable pain for many years. Nearly half of the adult population suffered from osteoarthritis and other degenerative diseases of the bones. Arthritis occurred most commonly in the back (amongst both adults and children), possibly as a result of regularly carrying heavy loads. No

37 *The Neolithic stone houses at Knap of Howar, Orkney.*

more than 2 per cent of the population had suffered broken bones, indicating that accidents or violence were only very rarely a cause of death. However, life expectancy was short. Many children died in infancy and few people lived to over 50. The average expectation of 15-year-olds is calculated as a further 9 years for women and 13 years for men. However, recent work on nineteenth-century skeletons has shown that archaeologists have consistently underestimated people's age at death. In other words, people probably lived far longer than the estimates for Isbister and Quanterness suggest.

Life was not exactly easy but it was nothing like the skin-clad, club-carrying caricature that has influenced popular perceptions of prehistory. Images of prehistoric life as primitive, brutish and short have been so pervasive that many people have had trouble ascribing any sophistication to these people. Another discovery has changed our attitudes to these people's level of technological and intellectual sophistication. Many of their ceremonial monuments in the Later Neolithic display an awareness of the movements of the sun and moon. They were certainly astronomers, but probably not to the elaborate extent that some have claimed.

Alternative visions of the past conceive of lost 'Golden Ages'; times when people lived closer to nature and harnessed forces and abilities which have been lost or neglected in modern urban and industrial life. The idea of the noble savage, uncorrupted and in harmony with the true values of humanity, has been around since the ancient Greeks. Our own myth of a noble and wondrous past has been sustained by many people, including those who believe in ley-lines and earth forces, who see the monuments of prehistory as misunderstood by the academics.

There has been little compromise between the theories of the ley-line believers and the archaeologists. The two camps are firmly divided. The discovery by archaeologists of significant solar and lunar alignments for Neolithic and Bronze Age monuments, including some long distance alignments, has in many ways borne out some of the claims of the ley-hunters. Nevertheless, there are still major disagreements about the more spectacular claims for long-distance lines of energy and a prehistoric science of geomancy, as advocated by ley-hunters. Archaeologists themselves are not immune to myths about the past. Most consider that they are uncovering evidence rather than imposing a preconceived vision upon it. Some wish only to present the bare facts of their discoveries. Others try to interpret what they and others have found, to enable people to share in the excitement of discovery.

There is a growing realization that no one can escape the constraints of society's value systems to be able to write an entirely unbiased and objective account of the past. But it should make us all the more determined to recognize our myths and values woven into those accounts, and to spot them in the works of others.

3

Geometry in the landscape

During a violent storm in Orkney in 1867, a large sand dune was washed away, exposing the remains of a hitherto undiscovered and unbelievably well preserved village at Skara Brae, some 5300 years old (**38**). The site has been excavated and is now open to the public. The stone houses provide us with another tantalizing glimpse of life all those millennia ago.

A few years ago, the archaeologist Colin Richards was carrying out a field survey to find settlements similar to Skara Brae. He had walked the fields over many square kilometres of Orkney, looking for chipped stone in the ploughsoil, but with little success. One cold autumn day in the few hours of daylight, his assistant, Miranda Schofield, suggested that they look in the field next to the Stones of Stenness, an imposing prehistoric monument. Could it be that no one had thought to fieldwalk here before? As Colin paced along the grid that they had laid out, he noticed that Miranda was wandering in circles. Wondering why she was not walking along the grid, he went over to see what she was doing. She held out a handful of chipped stones, finally evidence of an undiscovered settlement (**39**).

The next spring, Colin Richards returned with a small team to dig a trench into the settlement. The area that they opened up produced a few small finds but no evidence at all of the stone houses that he thought were there. On the very last day, his dog Rufus got loose and began digging into a rabbit burrow on the edge of the loch. The dog became stuck in the hole and had to be pulled out by his tail. When the diggers looked in the hole they saw the wall of a prehistoric house. As Colin Richards and his team were to find out over the next few years, their exploratory trench was placed

exactly in the open space between the houses of a settlement of the same date as Skara Brae (**40**).

The houses of this settlement, called Barnhouse, were organized in a similar way to those at Skara Brae. Although Barnhouse was not so well preserved, we can reconstruct the appearance of the houses at both sites. A low and narrow doorway led into a windowless room, lit only by the firelight from a central hearth. On entering the house, people moved to the right of the hearth, past a stone bedframe. Opposite the doorway was a large stone dresser (**41**). Another bed was located on the left-hand side of the entrance (**42**). In the later phase at Skara

38 *The Neolithic village of Skara Brae, Orkney.*

39 Excavations at Barnhouse. In the foreground is the house with two hearths.

Brae and at Barnhouse the bed spaces were recessed into the walls. Recent analyses of the phosphate levels inside the houses at Barnhouse indicate that there were higher levels by the left bed than by the right. Phosphate is present in, among other things, urine and perhaps indicates where the babies and young children were nursed by their mothers. The man's bed would thus be nearest the door.

Not all the houses conformed to this layout. At Skara Brae one house, isolated from the others, contained no beds. The house had been used for heating and cracking rocks to make into stone tools; it is referred to as a workshop but it could also have had a special social significance, such as a men's house. A second unusual house at Skara Brae had its own passage leading up to it; all the other houses were connected by another narrow, covered passage which ran the length of the settlement. When the site was excavated, this was the only house which had been left like a time capsule,

with objects still positioned where they had last been used. There were beads and bone points scattered across the room and pots had been left where they had sat. On the left-hand bed was the skull of a small bull. This house had a door which opened from the outside and not from the inside, unlike all the others. It seems to have been used for keeping people in rather than out. There was another curious feature. The corpses of two women had been buried under the floor. What was the significance of this structure? Was it a shrine, a strongroom or a place of retreat? Perhaps it was used by women as a place of confinement during menstruation, a practice found in many societies today.

The two settlements had other unusual features. Skara Brae (43) was constructed with large quantities of refuse packed inside the cavity walls. The same was probably true at Barnhouse but only the bases of the walls have survived there. Perhaps the reason for this was to provide sufficient insulation during the long winter months. Both villages also had elaborate and sophisticated drainage systems. Covered stone-lined channels led waste away from the houses to collecting areas. We might

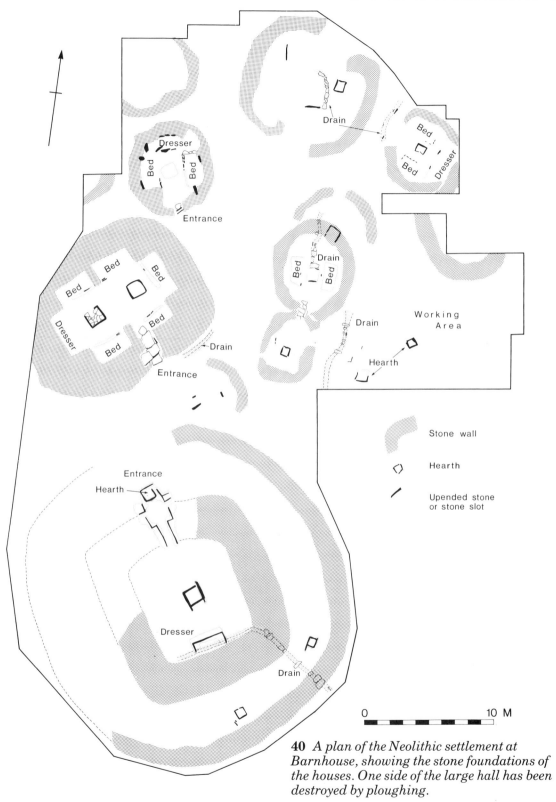

40 *A plan of the Neolithic settlement at Barnhouse, showing the stone foundations of the houses. One side of the large hall has been destroyed by ploughing.*

Stone wall

Hearth

Upended stone or stone slot

0   10 M

41 *The stone dresser and other internal features of House 7 at Skara Brae, in Orkney.*

42 *A stone box bed at Skara Brae.*

interpret this as a way of expelling sewage but what we are probably looking at is a very effective way of collecting manure for use on the fields as fertilizer.

Barnhouse had further surprises in store. Two buildings were much bigger than the others. One was essentially a double house with two hearths, while the other was a large rectangular building with rounded corners, set within a high stone wall. The double house had ordinary household refuse on its floors but the large building had been kept clean. What were they used for?

To begin to find out we have to consider the houses in relation to the tombs. The Orcadian tombs of this period seem to have been modelled on house interiors. Many tombs were 'stalled' like the Knap of Howar houses, while others were entered by a long passage, leading into a central chamber, with side chambers (equivalent to bed recesses in houses) leading off it. Two large tombs, at Quanterness and Quoyness, had the same layout as the double house at Barnhouse. The large 'hall' building at Barnhouse was unlike any tomb in its shape. However, it was built on an artificial platform of soil and surrounded by a large stone wall, both features of the great tomb at Maes Howe, with the largest chamber of its age in northern Europe. The north-facing entrance of the 'hall', through the stone wall, where several outdoor hearths were placed, faced directly towards Maes Howe. There is no doubt that the construc-

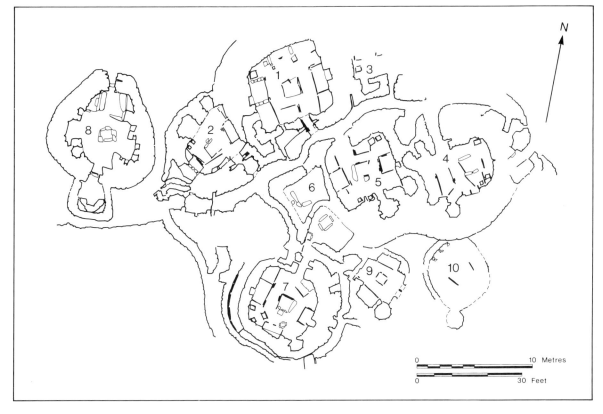

N

0   10 Metres

0   30 Feet

43 *A plan of the settlement at Skara Brae, Orkney.*

tion of all the Orcadian tombs and especially Maes Howe was a considerable achievement. The building of Maes Howe alone would have required 50,000–80,000 hours of labour. A hundred people would have worked for up to three months. Some archaeologists consider that such organization would have only been possible in a hierarchical society led by chiefs or by priests. For them the discovery of the double house was confirmation of that social order. It was the home of a chieftain's family over perhaps hundreds of years. Maybe. But it could also have served as the residence of two family groups who had decided to share their resources and bring the two hearths into one building. The hall no doubt had some ceremonial purpose but whether it was a chief's audience chamber or the village hall, we cannot tell.

While Colin Richards was studying the houses at Skara Brae and Barnhouse he noticed that the hearths, very solid rectangular stone troughs, all shared the same alignment, even though the doors of the houses faced in different directions. On closer analysis, he discovered that they were aligned on four important solar directions; midsummer sunrise and sunset, and midwinter sunrise and sunset. Orkney is the only place in the British Isles where these four directions are perpendicular to each other, thus forming a cross. It may well have been considered a very special place. He also discovered that the entrance to the large hall at Barnhouse, marked by a hearth in the doorway itself, was aligned on the midsummer sunset.

Mapping the heavens on the earth
The tomb of Maes Howe (**45**) also incorporates this concern with the sun's path. Almost all the other Orkney tombs faced to the east and the rising sun. At some time around 3600–3300 BC some of the largest tombs were constructed with a more complex rationale behind their orientation. Maes Howe's passage entrance faced to the south-west. On midwinter's day the dying sun still shines its rays along the passage and into the chamber, just as it sets. Perhaps

the Orcadians considered that the sun's death on the day of longest darkness was the herald of its rebirth in the next annual cycle. It was presumably also intimately linked to the hall at Barnhouse, a structure which celebrated midsummer for the living. The passage of the sun and the cycle of the seasons were thus fixed in the buildings (**46**).

The great tombs at the Bend in the Boyne in Ireland similarly deviate from the standard east-facing alignment. The great tomb at Knowth is surrounded by a group of small passage graves which all faced towards it. Its two passages, facing west and east, admit the rays of the sunrise at the spring and autumn equinoxes. Nearby at Newgrange the passage entrance is surmounted by a light box, a stone window which enables the light from the midwinter sunrise to shine all the way down the passage to the back wall of the burial chamber. There is another large tomb in the same group, at Dowth, but it was poorly excavated many years ago and we do not know whether it formed another component of this system of solar mapping (**47**). The Irish passage graves and those of north Wales, western Scotland and one site in Orkney at Pierowall (see **64**) are

44 *(Above) Inside a Neolithic house at Skara Brae.*

45 *(Below) The great chambered tomb of Maes Howe, Orkney. The ditch and bank around it are also Neolithic.*

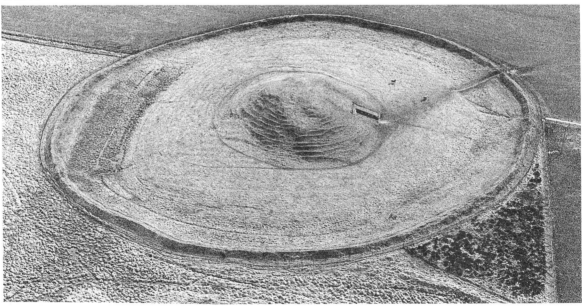

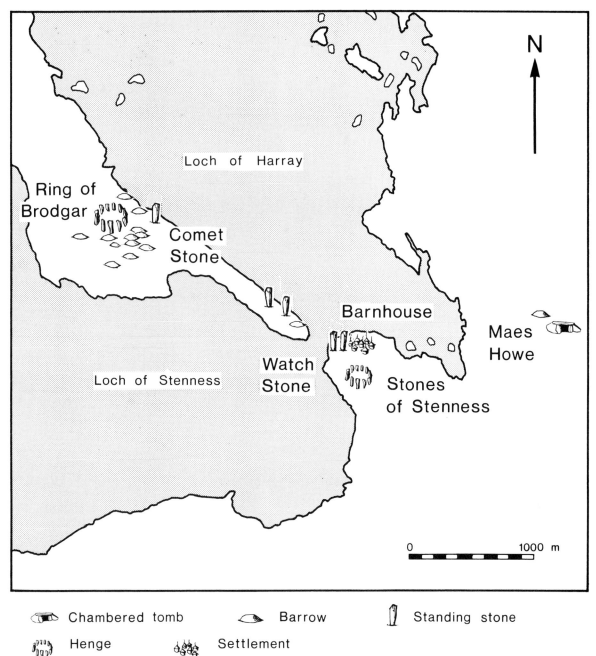

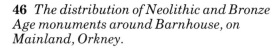

46 *The distribution of Neolithic and Bronze Age monuments around Barnhouse, on Mainland, Orkney.*

famous for their magnificent carved friezes of spirals and circles. Some of these elaborately carved stones sat at the front of the tombs and others were incorporated into the passages. Curiously, some designs were deliberately hid-

den. At Knowth some stones had their carved sides incorporated into the chamber walls so that the motifs could not be seen.

In southern Britain and the Midlands people were building a very different kind of monument at this time. We call this class of site a 'cursus', after William Stukeley, an antiquarian of the eighteenth century, who thought they were used for prehistoric horse-

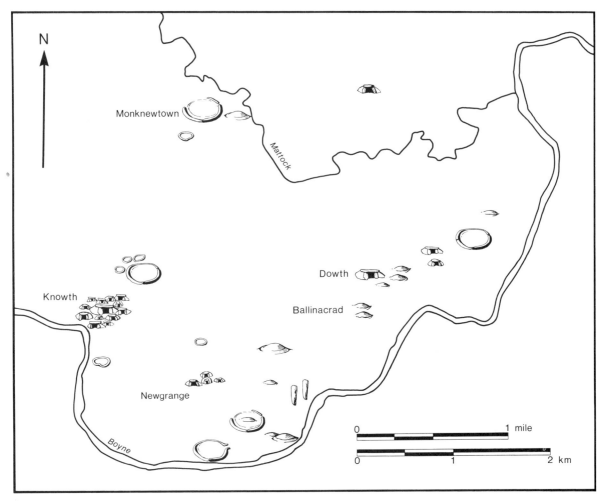

47 *The distribution of Neolithic tombs and henges in the Bend in the Boyne, Ireland.*

and chariot-racing. They are parallel-sided, with ditches often 100 or more metres (328 ft) apart, which may run from over 1 km up to 10 km (0.6 to 6 miles), terminating in rectangular or rounded ends (**48**). They tend to be oriented approximately either north-west to south-east or north-east to south-west. At Dorchester-on-Thames (Oxfordshire) the line of a smaller enclosure and a barrow was slighted and overlaid by a cursus (**49**). Archaeologists have discovered that the earlier alignment faced the minor moonrise (the smallest arc of the moon's rising) at midsummer, an orientation which occurs only once during the moon's long cycle (the lunar cycle takes 18.61 years to complete). In contrast, the west end of the later

cursus faced the midsummer sunset. Similarly astronomical correspondences have been noticed for other cursus monuments. The cursus next to Stonehenge forms an alignment with Woodhenge, a timber circle half a mile away. This alignment leads to a major bend in the river Avon and coincides with the direction of sunrise at the spring and autumn equinoxes.

The largest cursus of all is the Dorset cursus (see **51**) which runs for 10 km (6 miles). It is not straight but curves northwards. The earliest section, in the middle stretch of the monument,

48 *The southern end of Cursus A at Rudston (Yorkshire), now ploughed flat and visible as a soilmark. The end of the terminal is at the bottom centre of the picture and the cursus runs close to the modern road, which crosses it in the upper right-hand side of the picture.*

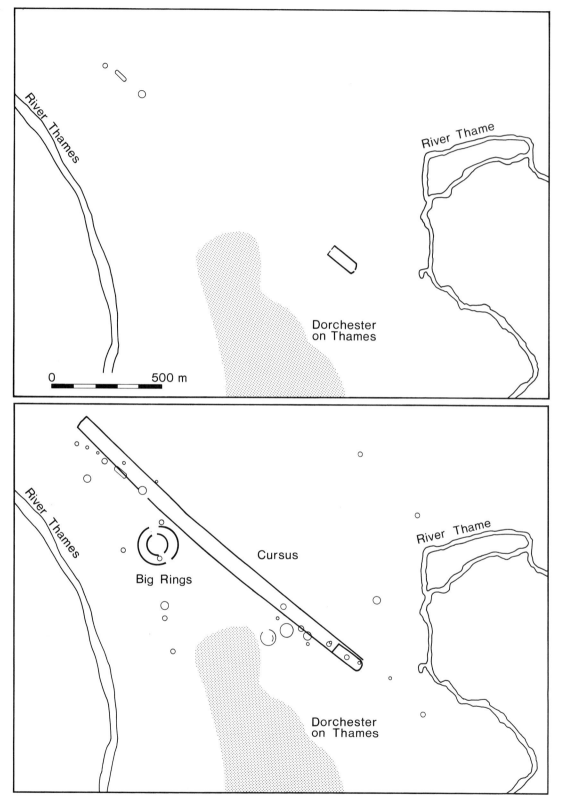

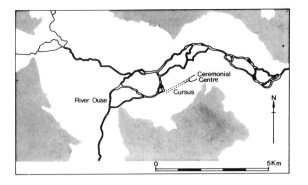

50 *The ceremonial monument at Godmanchester (Cambridgeshire). The cursus was added later and stops at the back of the monument. The enclosure, and probably the two ring ditches, are Bronze Age. The (?) shrine and (?) temple are probably much later in date.*

faced west towards the midwinter sunset, with the sun setting behind an earlier long barrow, incorporated into one end of the cursus. The purpose of cursuses is still something of a mystery. The Dorset cursus had banks of chalk along its sides which originally stood to a height of 2 m (6½ ft). It ran over hilly ground, part of which was wooded (which we know from the species of woodland snails found in its ditch). It was not possible to see from one end to the other. Many other cursuses have been found by aerial photography on the gravel terraces of the major rivers of southern Britain. The precision with which they were laid out is sometimes astonishing. At Godmanchester (Cambridgeshire), a cursus was aligned on one side of an earlier, huge enclosure 350 m (1148 ft) long and 230 m (755 ft) wide (**50**). Inside the ditch were 24 carefully positioned large posts. Six of their intersections correspond with solstice or equinoctial positions of the sun and moon. It is unlikely that these correspondences are accidental, but archaeologists are still speculating about the purpose of the post settings. Most astonishingly, the posts were put up by 3800 BC, hundreds of years

49 *The development of the ceremonial landscape at Dorchester-on-Thames (Oxfordshire). An alignment of monuments for lunar observances (above) was replaced by a solar aligned cursus. The monument served as a focus for Late Neolithic and Early Bronze Age round barrows (below).*

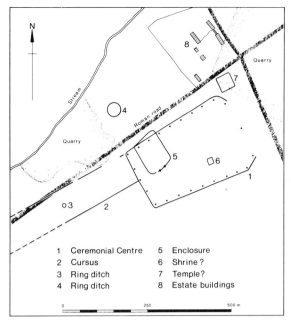

1	Ceremonial Centre	5	Enclosure
2	Cursus	6	Shrine ?
3	Ring ditch	7	Temple?
4	Ring ditch	8	Estate buildings

earlier than any other known monument incorporating astronomical bearings.

Some, if not all, of the cursuses had astronomical functions. Their placing within the landscape also shows that they were linked in special ways to the land. The Dorset cursus (**51**) divided a densely inhabited upland area from a lowland area, sparsely occupied other than by a large ceremonial henge complex at Knowlton (of a slightly later date). Many of the other cursuses are found in groups of two or three in the same place. A recent discovery at Goldington, near Bedford, is of a group of at least five small cursuses (or long enclosures), of varying shapes, sizes and orientations (**52**). The Cleaver Dyke in Scotland is perhaps the best preserved cursus. In parts its bank stands to nearly 2 m (6½ ft). Cursuses may have been used as ceremonial gathering places and some have produced human bones. Like the long barrows and other tombs, these were architectural monuments which allowed people to relate the movements of the heavens to particular places on the earth. Cursuses are normally dated to around 3000 BC but the Drayton cursus in Oxfordshire has recently produced a date of 3635–3385 BC, contemporary with the causewayed enclosures and earlier tombs. Their period of use was also contemporary with the circular ditched enclosures known as henges. In some cases, such as the Dorset cursus, they

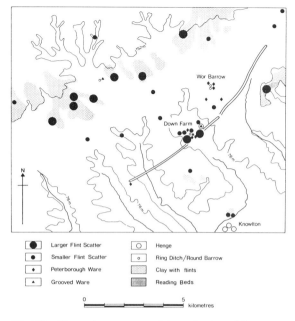

Larger Flint Scatter
Smaller Flint Scatter
Peterborough Ware
Grooved Ware
Henge
Ring Ditch/Round Barrow
Clay with flints
Reading Beds

0   5
kilometres

51 *The Dorset cursus and its relationship to Late Neolithic settlements.*

provided a focus or structure for the location of monuments and settlements in the landscape for many centuries after their construction.

Reordering the landscape

While the areas where these monuments were built had become increasingly deforested, other regions were reverting to woodland from around 3500–3300 BC. Many of the more marginal soils seem to have been deserted and people retreated to the core areas. From the distribution of axes of this period, we know that communities had withdrawn to the more productive areas. These were the more fertile soils of the Boyne, Orkney, eastern Scotland, Anglesey, the upper Thames, Wessex, Essex, Yorkshire and the river valleys of the Wash. On the open chalklands of southern Britain, arable cultivation appears to have ceased and large tracts were used only as pasture. In the Somerset Levels trackways were again being built across the marshes; some woodland areas were still being exploited, but as managed woodland rather than land to be cleared. In the core areas there is also evidence for intensification of agricultural production. At Fengate, ditched paddocks were laid out to form an intricate system of cattle enclosures. In the Milfield Basin (Northumberland) lines of pits

seem to have been dug and used to divide up the land. The settlements of Skara Brae and Barnhouse also represent a change in land use on Orkney. Settlement now concentrated on the difficult but ultimately more fertile soils. These needed considerable community effort to drain and bring into cultivation. Perhaps this was why these villages appear so tightly knit. There is also evidence of the use of the plough in western Europe at this time. Whereas the ard merely scratches a furrow in the soil, the plough actually turns the soil, creating better conditions for plant growth. Ploughing would have made possible more intensive cultivation than ard and spade tillage. Around the world today, ploughs are used in societies where most of the agricultural labour is done by men. Women do most of the work in the fields in societies characterized by hoe agriculture. Perhaps the widespread adoption of the plough gave men a more dominant role in agricultural production, and in social matters generally.

After over a thousand years of early farming, a way of life based on ancestral tombs, forest clearance and settlement expansion came to an end. This was a time of important social changes. In southern Britain, many tombs were deliberately blocked up by c. 3200 BC and the ditches of the causewayed enclosures had also silted up by this time. Certain enclosures developed clear defensive characteristics and archaeologists have excavated at least four which had been attacked. A way of life was coming to an end but a new lifestyle was emerging in the consolidated heartlands. Perhaps the loss of fertility in the more marginal lands had shaken beliefs in the powers of the ancestors to ensure the success of the crops. Recent research on the alignments of long barrows and other tombs suggests that, in 90 per cent of cases, their entrances faced not the rising sun but the rising moon. Some archaeologists have suggested that monuments which celebrated the moon were increasingly abandoned or replaced by monuments that marked the passage of the sun. Perhaps new divine forces, embodied by the sun, were now considered to safeguard harvests and the reproduction of the clans and the herds.

Circles of stone and timber

The Barnhouse settlement lies next to the Stones of Stenness, a circle which originally comprised 12 tall stones, inside a bank and ditch

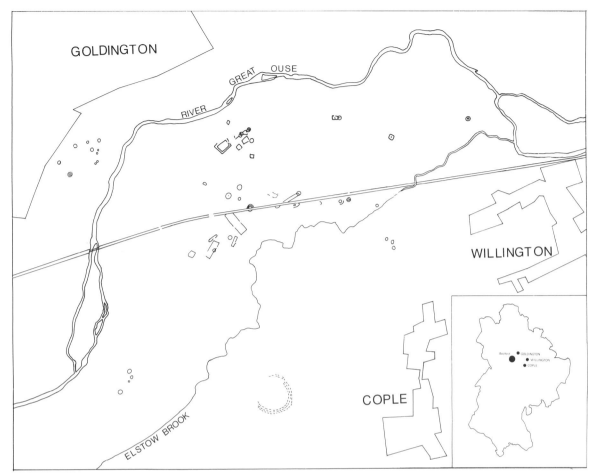

GOLDINGTON

RIVER GREAT OUSE

WILLINGTON

COPLE

ELSTOW BROOK

52 *The small cursuses or long mortuary enclosures and ring ditches at Goldington, Bedford, visible as cropmarks.*

and surrounding a giant-sized hearth. This monument may have been built at the same time or up to 300 years after the settlement, around 3000 BC. The Stones of Stenness were one of the first circles to be built, the beginning of a tradition which lasted over a thousand years and which was almost entirely confined to the British Isles, with a few exceptions such as the stone circle at Er Lannic in Brittany. Many hundreds of stone circles were constructed in the upland regions of Britain and Ireland. Circles of timber and even circles of pits were created in the lowland zones. A lowland example of a stone circle is Rollright (Oxfordshire), where the ring of stones was originally a continuous wall with just one narrow entrance to the southeast. Curiously, stone circles of this type are normally found only in Cumbria and eastern

Ireland. One of the most atmospheric of the Cumbrian circles is Castlerigg (**colour plate 9**), surrounded by spectacular mountain scenery. The stone circles were built in a variety of shapes and sizes. They were circular, ovoid, rectilinear or simply irregular. Some were only 10 m (33 ft) in diameter and others were enormous. The 60 or more stones, some over 5 m (16½ ft) high, that originally formed the Ring of Brodgar (**53**) next to Stenness, were encircled by a ditch, 3 m (10 ft) deep and over 100 m (329 ft) in diameter. Some circles incorporated straight lines of standing stones as at Beaghmore in Ireland. Many of the single standing stones were probably erected in the third millennium BC and the early part of the second millennium BC. There are many of these in the West Country, Ireland, Wales and Scotland. Notable examples are the Devil's Arrows at Boroughbridge (Yorkshire) and the Rudston monolith, now in a Yorkshire churchyard, close to the intersection of four cursuses (**54**).

53 *The Ring of Brodgar, Orkney.*

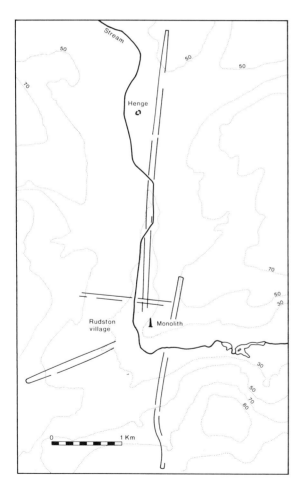

There has been a considerable amount of analysis and debate about these monuments. Alexander Thom, an engineer, proposed that they were built according to a 'megalithic yard'. He also set out to demonstrate that the people who built them were sophisticated astronomers, sighting the component stones of the circles on the movements of the sun, the moon, the stars and prominent landmarks. There is no doubt that the movements of the sun and the moon were important to these people, but evidence for plotting the movements of the stars is debatable. Our notions of scientific astronomy are probably very different from their conceptions of the cosmos.

There are no simple explanations. There seems to have been tremendous diversity not only between regions but also within them, perhaps unsurprising for a thousand-year fashion. The idea of a standard unit of measurement is very plausible but it was not as regular as some people have liked to think. It averages something just over 80 cm (31½ in), about the length of an adult's pace. As for the astronomical alignments, many circles do not seem to be sighted on any particular occurrence. In western Scotland many circles are sighted towards the south-east, the southern limit of the moon's rising. Others have pro-

54 *The Rudston cursuses. Within the modern village is the large standing stone, which may be later than the cursuses.*

55 *The Late Neolithic henge at Thornborough (Yorkshire). The circular bank survives but the inner and outer ditches are visible only as cropmarks. It is the middle one of three henges and was built on the line of a cursus (under its left side).*

duced solar alignments. Of course, there are many stone circles and other monuments which seem to have had no obvious astronomical purpose.

Stenness is also considered to be a henge. A henge is a circular earthwork with an exterior bank and an interior ditch (as if to keep some-thing inside rather than out) and two opposed entrances or one single entrance. Not all are perfectly circular. Some contained circles of pits, instead of posts or stones. 'Henge' is the term for the circular bank and ditch and not the stones or timbers inside it. A few are extremely well preserved, such as Arbor Low (Derbyshire) (see **81**) and one of the three henges at Thornborough, near Ripon (**55**), which is hidden in a wood. Henges vary considerably in size, from under 20 m (66 ft) in diameter to over 100 m (329 ft).

The name 'henge' comes from Stonehenge (probably from the Old English word meaning

56 *King Arthur's Round Table and Mayburgh; two henges near Penrith.*

'hanging') and archaeologists apply the word to similar sites. Curiously, Stonehenge is not a good example of a henge as the term is now used. The first phase of Stonehenge, which dates to *c*.3000 BC, looked very different to the way it does today. It was a circular ditch and bank with an entrance facing the midsummer sunrise. Unlike all the other henges, its bank was built inside the ditch rather than outside it. Within the ditch and bank was a circle of 56 pits. There may have been a circular wooden structure near the centre of the circle and five or six small standing stones. We must forget its large stones for the moment since these were not put up until some 800 years later. It was almost pathetically small in relation to the earlier Stonehenge cursus and the nearby henge enclosure, built around 2500 BC, at Durrington Walls (see **58**).

On the chalklands of Wessex are five henges whose banks and ditches are of considerable dimensions. These huge monuments are known as henge enclosures (containing a number of circular henge buildings inside the banked and ditched area). Probably the earliest was the great circle at Avebury, recently re-dated to *c*.3200 BC (**57** and **colour plate 7**). We do not know whether the standing stones placed within it and forming the Avenue leading to the south-west were erected at this time or some centuries later. A similarly large henge at Durrington Walls is perched in a low valley overlooking a prominent bend in the river Avon, on which the Stonehenge cursus is aligned. It contained a number of timber circles, up to 30 m (98 ft) in diameter, and was set next to a much smaller henge with its own timber circle, Woodhenge, which was aligned on the midsummer sunrise. These timber structures consisted of concentric rings of tree trunks which may have stood over 6 m (20 ft) high. We do not know whether they were roofed or whether they were open to the elements with perhaps cross braces at the tops. The work involved in felling and transporting and carpentry and erection of the timber circles was considerable – hundreds of mature trees were required. Digging the ditch at Durrington needed the equivalent of half a million hours of labour, or 1000 people working for several months (**58**).

57 *Reconstruction of the Sanctuary henge at Avebury.*

In the Milfield Basin (Northumberland) (**59**), there is a concentration of small henges, some linked by a cursus-like earthwork. One of these, at Yeavering, was the initial focus for subsequent ceremonial monuments and activities into the Bronze Age (**60**).

One of the most impressive monuments of the Later Neolithic, constructed around 2700 BC, is Silbury Hill near Avebury (**colour plate 3**). It was initially a relatively small round mound which was later considerably enlarged by means of a series of chalk cones, one on top of the other, to give a stepped appearance. It was a massive undertaking, involving over 3 million hours of labour. In other words, it would have taken 1000 workers nearly two years to construct, no doubt supported by a community five times that size or even larger. New discoveries half a mile away indicate that there was also a huge circular timber palisade in the

Kennet valley. This was 170 m (558 ft) in diameter and incorporated radial lines of posts as well as a double ring of posts inside, of 40 m (131 ft) diameter. Each post was about 0.5 m (1½ ft) in diameter and was set 2 m (6½ ft) into the ground. The whole structure may have stood 6 m (20 ft) high and formed an unbroken wall of 10,000 tree trunks. Avebury, already an area of many long barrows built over a thousand years before, was becoming an important ceremonial centre. Similar but smaller mounds have also been noted in close association to other henges in the region. Just what the relationship was has been the subject of some speculation, including the notion that these mounds represented a mother goddess. There is another large mound at Marlborough which was used as a Norman castle. There is some evidence that it might have existed well before the castle was built there. Is this a second Silbury Hill?

In some regions the monuments of the past were subsumed within the new order. The passage grave at Newgrange was encircled by a

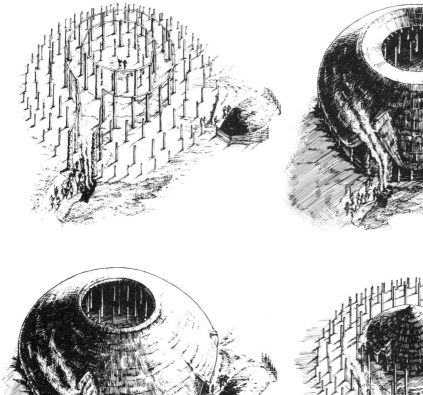

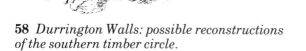

58 *Durrington Walls: possible reconstructions of the southern timber circle.*

ring of stones. Several cursuses were aligned on earlier long barrow tombs. But in most places the new monuments represented a total break with the old.

It may seem curious that the earliest example of the henge tradition is found in Orkney. We tend to see the islands of Orkney as marginal to the rest of the British Isles. But 5000 years ago Orkney was a very special place, perhaps because of its solar alignments. Not only is Stenness the earliest dated henge but a new form of pottery may well have originated in Orkney by 3300 BC. It is called Grooved Ware (**61**) because of its decoration and was the first pottery in Britain to have flat bases. Earlier styles were less decorated, if not plain,

and had rounded bases; they could not be set down on a flat surface, such as the stone 'dressers' of the Orkney houses, but could nestle in the ash bed of the cooking hearth. Within 500 years the fashion of Grooved Ware had spread throughout eastern Britain. It has been found in small quantities in Ireland and the far west of Britain, but seems never to have caught on in these western regions. The large henge monuments of the south used great quantities of Grooved Ware. It is predominantly found associated with the bones of one particular food animal: the pig. At Durrington Walls an extensive midden was discovered next to one of the circles, the remains of one or many feasts where large quantities of pork were eaten. Many archaeologists think that the prominence of pig bones means that the forests of the region had regenerated, since pigs thrive in woodland. But people's diets are not entirely

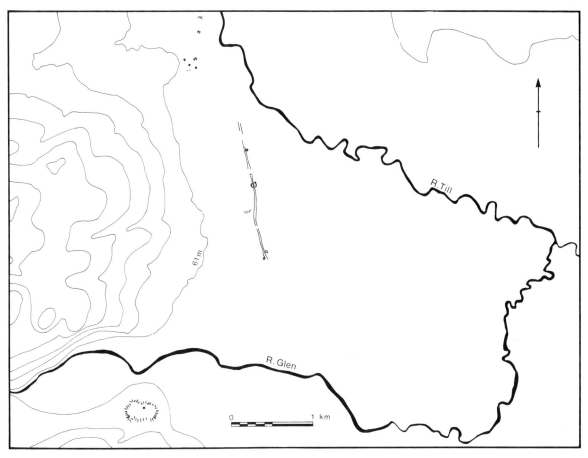

59 *The distribution of henges, a linear earthwork and pit alignments in the Milfield Basin (Northumberland).*

60 *The henge, Late Bronze Age cremation cemetery and standing stone at Yeavering, in the Milfield Basin. (Lower left of 59.)*

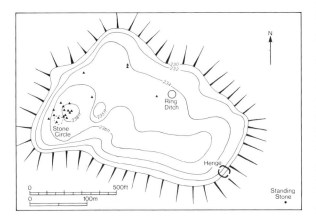

conditioned by their environment. The people of the henge enclosures may simply have had a preference for pork since it is a fine feasting food.

Grooved Ware was one of two main pottery styles in Britain up to 4500 years ago. The other, Peterborough Ware (with its sub-types Mortlake, Ebbsfleet and Fengate ware), was a round-bottomed style, decorated with impressions made with bird bones and twisted cord. Although they were contemporary, Grooved Ware and Peterborough Ware (**62**) were hardly ever used together, even though they were present in the same areas. Peterborough pots were occasionally placed as offerings in rivers. In contrast, Grooved Ware has entirely different associations. It occurs in the henge monuments and within a few kilometres of them. It is also associated with higher quality arrowheads and greater numbers of axes. In Dorchester a henge monument at Mount Pleasant (with Grooved Ware) is situated immediately next to a large, circular interrupted ditch enclosure, at

61 *Grooved Ware pottery.*

Flagstones, which produced a small quantity of Peterborough Ware. The two monuments are probably contemporary yet the pottery styles are completely different. We do not know how to account for this. Were they the property of two different tribes which were intermingled across the land? Were they the trappings of a henge-using caste or class and a henge-building underclass? Or were they simply used for different occasions or at different times of the year?

The enclosure at Flagstones has also produced some of the earliest graffiti in Britain. On several of the vertical surfaces of a chalk-cut ditch are crude carvings (**63**). One of them is an amorphous but roughly circular shape. Its poor execution contrasts with the carving in the passage graves and with the relatively precise chevrons and straight lines (very much Grooved Ware styles) which are common graffiti in the village at Skara Brae. Orkney is unusual because it is the meeting place of two artistic styles which otherwise were never used in the same region. The eastern part of Britain used Grooved Ware styles of straight lines and chevrons on its pottery and other artefacts. North Wales and Ireland were characterized by a different design style called 'passage grave art' (spirals, circles and other forms pecked into the rock with stone pounders). Only in Orkney do both styles occur together (**64**). Another art style seems to have appeared at this time, mainly in northern England and Scotland. These are known as 'cup-and-ring marks' (**65**) and were pounded into the surfaces of stone slabs. Some are found at stone circles, as at Clava, and others at prominent natural landmarks. The rings, spirals and cup marks are

62 *A small Peterborough Ware bowl.*

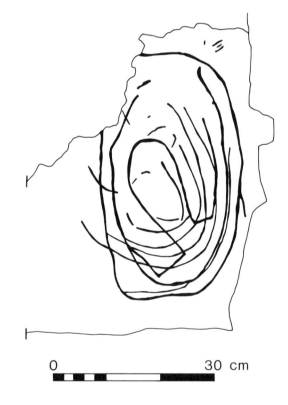

63 *The Late Neolithic graffiti from the enclosure at Flagstones, Dorchester.*

64 *The decorated stone from a chambered tomb at Pierowall quarry, Westray, Orkney.*

65 *Cup-and-ring marks carved on a rock-face at Ballygowan, Argyll.*

very simple in comparison to passage grave art, though cup marks are found in that style at Newgrange. However, cup-and-ring was a pan-European style, found from central Europe to Scandinavia to Iberia. We still know very little about these art forms and what they represented.

67 *The grave goods from the Late Neolithic burial at Liff's Low, Derbyshire. The antler macehead was found below the man's feet and the rest were found above his head, in the arrangement shown.*

66 *The distribution of Later Neolithic axe quarries and mines.*

Prestigious goods and the search for novelty

Many of the earlier axe production sites stopped making axes at the onset of the forest regeneration phase, after 3300 BC. A few like Langdale, Land's End and Graig Llydd actually increased production. The manufacture of stone and flint tools, including axes, seems to have become more centralized (**66**). At Grimes Graves in East Anglia many hundreds of mining shafts were sunk deep into the ground, over an area of 4 ha (9 acres) to extract the good quality flint that lay at that level (**colour plates 4** and **5**). The shafts that have been investigated show that the extracted flint was made into axes and small, disc-shaped knives. These are thought to have been exchanged over wide areas of the country but curiously we do not know where these products went. They do not turn up in large quantities locally. Over 4000 tons of flint were extracted from about five hundred shafts. At the bases of the shafts the miners cut galleries with picks of deer antler and stone axes. Two of these axes were not local products, as we might expect, but had

come all the way from Cornwall. The blade of one could be matched with blade marks on the chalk face.

Archaeologists used to think that the large-scale and specialized production of axes from Grimes Graves would have had profound effects on tree clearance throughout Britain. As many as five million axes could have been made from the flint, with each shaft taking 15 people three months to dig. But a detailed analysis of the flint debris from one of the shafts demonstrated that the production of axes was not a central concern of the miners. They were making all kinds of tools. This was not the hyper-specialized industry that everyone had thought. There was other evidence that flint extraction was not the rational industrial process that many archaeologists have assumed. From a shaft excavated some years ago came indications that offerings were made: on the floor of the shaft was a pile of flint covered by antlers. One gallery had failed to locate any flint and at its entrance was placed a pregnant female figurine of carved chalk, together with a chalk phallus and two chalk balls. If these artefacts are not modern forgeries, and there is a suspicion that they might be, they seem to suggest that the chalk itself was regarded as a being or force whose bounty, or fertility, could not be assured.

The products of these flint mines were sometimes beautifully flaked and polished. They are some of the many rather special artefacts which were in circulation and which were occasionally placed in graves (**67**). Boars' tusks, very thin flint axes, other types of polished flint tools, unusually fine pottery bottles, bone pins and necklaces were among these special items and they began to appear as grave goods with individual burials after 3000 BC. Although cremation had been practised in some regions in the preceding millennium, it became much more widespread. The small henge which was to become Stonehenge was later used as a small cremation cemetery and many of the burials contained these new and special items. In the search for such novelties, people began to expand their exchange links. By 2500 BC the technology to create metal had arrived in the British Isles.

4

The first metals

In 1986 English Heritage's Central Excavation Unit, their roving field team, was excavating a group of four round mounds on an island in the river Nene near Irthlingborough (**68**). A large part of the valley was being exploited for gravel extraction and three of the mounds would soon be destroyed. One of the largest mounds had been rebuilt twice, each time larger than before. Much later, some centuries after it was built, it was reused for cremation burials (probably around 1800 BC), but the greatest surprise was the burial deposit at its centre. As Clare Halpin's team of excavators carefully trowelled away the soil on the top of the mound, they came to a layer of poorly preserved bone above and within the remains of a limestone cairn (**69**). The acid gravel soil had eaten away the less robust pieces of bone over the last 4500 years, leaving a delicate lacework of rotted bone which had to be recorded three-dimensionally and carefully lifted. The bone layer and the stones had slumped into a depression. A wooden structure had stood here, incorporating a chamber. As the wood had rotted, thousands of years ago, so the layers above fell into the void. In the chamber lay a human skeleton. Another burial had been placed in a separate grave pit before the mound was built and probably around the same time as the first burial. This second, crouched burial turned out to be an adult, probably a male, and was accompanied by a single grave good, a bone needle. The first burial was that of an adult male, laid out on his side and partly disarticulated (**70**). He was equipped with a variety of goods. There was a pottery beaker, 12 flints (including an arrowhead that had never been used), an archer's wristguard of stone (reused as a tool, probably for polishing), as well as five jet buttons, an amber ring, two carved pieces of cow's ribs (thin bone spatulae), two finger-shaped stones (one of soft chalk and the other of hard greenstone), a boar's tusk and a beautiful dagger made entirely out of flint. Microscopic analysis of the surfaces of the dagger's blade showed that, like the arrowhead, it had never been used. There was no trace of the tiny scratch marks (known as microwear) which show that a flint tool has been used.

When the first stages of the analyses of the burial deposit were complete, a number of intriguing questions emerged. Why were the remains of the man with grave goods disarticulated? Even his lower jaw was missing. Had his body been disturbed in the grave or had he been dead for some time before he was placed in the chamber? There had also been a wooden superstructure over the chamber, suggesting that his tomb had a small shrine or viewing platform above it. The bone layer had consisted of the remains of cattle (see **69**). These remains had derived from about 184 cattle skulls, 38 mandibles, 33 shoulder blades and 15 pelvises. These had been stacked up, probably five high, on the top of the mound, covering the limestone cairn.

The man's grave goods indicate that he or his mourners had connections across large areas of eastern England. The jet had come from Whitby in Yorkshire, the flint dagger from

68 *The round barrow at Irthlingborough (Northamptonshire) under excavation.*

69 *The deposit of cattle skulls and other bones at Irthlingborough.*

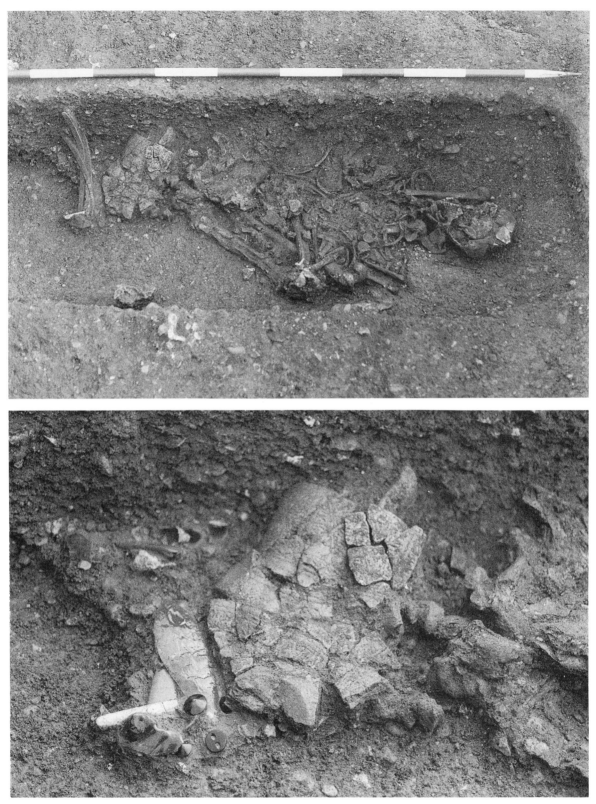

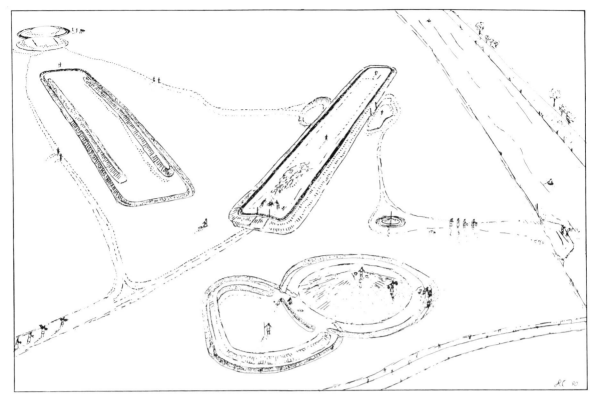

71 *Reconstruction of the Early Bronze Age landscape at West Cotton, incorporating monuments from earlier centuries.*

East Anglia, and the chalk lumps from Wessex. In addition, the amber ring came from the Baltic Sea region. The ages of the cattle could be ascertained from their teeth. Most were around two years old and probably male. These bullocks were at their prime for meat yield. Either these beasts were part of a single cattle herd or they were brought together from many different herds from all over the region, presumably to be consumed at a funeral feast. Some of the teeth and a horn came from the skull of an aurochs, the wild species of cattle that had been living in Britain since the end of the last Ice Age. The last occurrence of this animal before its extinction in Britain was nine hundred years later; it was presumably becoming rare and may well have been ranched as a

70 *The primary grave pit at Irthlingborough, with the partially disarticulated skeleton and (below) a close-up of the grave goods.*

semi-domesticate. Alternatively it was a prized trophy, hunted in the wild.

We will never know who these men were. No other burial mound of this period (2600–1900 BC) was capped by a stack of cattle skulls. Was this the only funerary event where cattle were eaten in great numbers or were the skulls and other left-overs normally disposed of well away from the burial mound? Another aurochs skull had been found in a similar burial at Snail Down (Wiltshire) while occasional cattle skulls have been found in other burials. The grave goods are similar to many other sets from burials in southern Britain. A couple of kilometres further down the valley, at West Cotton (**71**), a similar mound produced another central burial of a man with a beaker-shaped pot, a flint dagger (**72** and see **34**), a jet button, a flint knife and a chalk implement. Burials such as Irthlingborough and West Cotton were by no means the richest; others (such as Barnack, further east near Peterborough) have been known to include small items of gold, such as basket-shaped 'earrings' (more probably hair-twists) and gold buttons, or stone battle axes (shaped like their metal prototypes in Central Europe, with a hafting hole through the middle).

72 *The flint dagger with the West Cotton burial.*

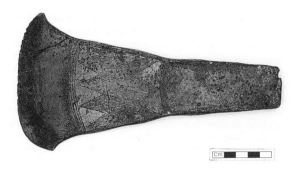

73 *One of the earliest bronze axes in Britain. Note the geometric incised decoration.*

The first uses of metal

A bronze axe was discovered in the ditch fills of the henge monument at Mount Pleasant in Dorchester, while the site was being excavated in 1971. Archaeologists were amazed: a 'Bronze Age' implement had been found on a site of the 'Stone Age'. In the first silts of the ditch were pottery sherds of Grooved Ware, dated to 2500 BC. The axe, of a style common in Ireland, had been deposited in the ditch just above these layers (**73**). An associated radiocarbon date came out at *c.*2300 BC. This was slightly earlier than the date of a large defensive palisade of timber trunks which was set up inside the area enclosed by the partly silted ditch. The deposition of the axe probably occurred between the uses of the monument as a henge and as a palisaded enclosure. From other British sites it was soon clear that the working of metal was happening at the same time as the final 'Stone Age' phase.

Although no metal was deposited in the Irthlingborough grave, we know that these people knew of the use of copper to make tools and weapons. The person who made the flint dagger (see **70b**) was copying a copper prototype. The battle axes found in other burials were also copies, not of copper axes, but of stone ones from northern and central Europe, which in turn were copies of copper originals. From northern Britain there are also a few stone copies of ordinary copper axes (or flat axes as they are called). The earliest gold and copper artefacts in Britain date from *c.*2700–2000 BC. Gold had been worked into trinkets in the Near East since 4500 BC and copper axes and tools

had been manufactured in the Balkans since 4600 BC. The inhabitants of the British Isles were backward in this respect, marginal peoples a whole continent away from the places of innovation. Two thousand years after copper was first mined in south-east Europe, people in Britain were copying in flint the tools of copper which they had seen. It is likely that copper axes and daggers were circulating in Britain but were too prized to be buried with the dead. People were certainly in touch with Europe and, as with the introduction of farming, the earliest copperworking seems to have been in Ireland. Copper axes of a distinctive Irish style have been found throughout Ireland, and are similar to continental forms. A recent discovery of a wooden trackway at Corlea, in Ireland, has also provided further evidence of early metal use. The timbers were felled between 2268 and 2251 BC and the axe marks appear to be those of a metal tool.

The manufacture of bronze was a technique which arrived in the British Isles not long after knowledge of copper metallurgy. While many other parts of Europe had a long period of using pure copper unmixed with other metals, the British Isles were so far behind that there was no discernible 'Copper Age' on these islands. Bronze is made by alloying copper with tin in a ratio of eight parts to one. If too much tin is added then the alloy shines like silver. Bronze is harder than copper; indeed the earliest copper tools were not markedly superior to stone. Before people in eastern Europe realized that tin could be added to copper, they used arsenic as a hardening alloy. Presumably the lifespan of arsenical bronzeworkers was short.

The earliest copper and bronze artefacts in Britain were axes, daggers and awls. There were also curious items called halberds, dagger-shaped blades which were fixed perpendicularly to handles like an axe. This form was common in the western Mediterranean and was probably first copied in the British Isles in Ireland, along with the flat axe. Many of these earliest metal tools and weapons were never used or sharpened. Some were too large for practical use. Their prime use seems to have been as status symbols, carried about and displayed. Although Britain was rich in copper and tin, its inhabitants were backward in comparison to the rest of Europe. Not only did they use copper much later than everyone else, but they used metal in very small quantities at first.

5 MINING AND MANUFACTURING METALS

The western regions of the British Isles are rich in metal ores. Tin, copper and silver have been mined in the south-west of Britain. Gold was mined in Wales in the Roman period, while Ireland has long been known for its deposits of gold and copper. It is very difficult to find prehistoric mines and quarries since they have been so often destroyed by later extraction. However, archaeologists have located some early copper mines at Mount Gabriel in southern Ireland and at the Great Orme in Wales. Those at Mount Gabriel were short tunnels dipping downwards and opening up into a large chamber where the ore deposits were more prolific. The Great Orme mine was a more elaborate system of horizontal and vertical tunnels, dug out to a depth of 70 m (230 ft) below ground. It was probably one of the largest copper mines in Europe. The ore was

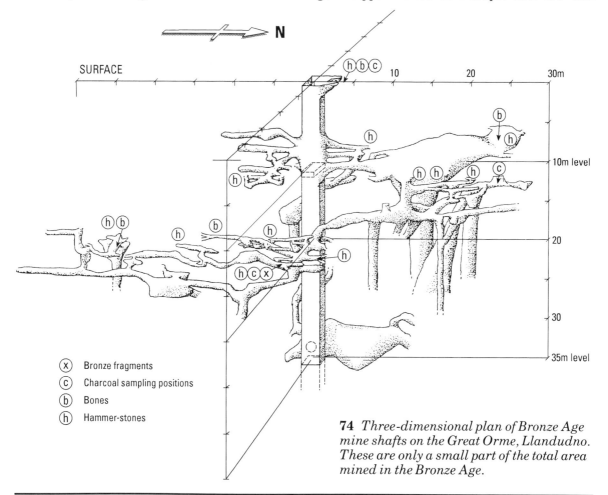

x Bronze fragments
c Charcoal sampling positions
b Bones
h Hammer-stones

74 *Three-dimensional plan of Bronze Age mine shafts on the Great Orme, Llandudno. These are only a small part of the total area mined in the Bronze Age.*

extracted by fire setting. Fires were lit underground and water was thrown on the rock to crack it. The fractured stone was then detached and possibly crushed by large beach cobbles which may have been fastened in wooden slings. Bone points were also used to gouge out the softer deposits within the rock. Charcoal samples from the fire settings have been radiocarbon dated to between 1800 and 600 BC. Some aspects of the mining process seem hard to explain in practical terms. The cobbles showed little or no signs of wear and tear and there were large quantities of animal bones from food remains left in the tunnels. An interesting detail about some of these tunnels is that they are too small for adults to move in unless they are potholers. If the mining was not done by dwarves (and there is no evidence for this at all!) then some may have been done by children.

A dozen prehistoric mines are known in south-west Ireland, in Cork and Kerry. A date from charcoal found in a mine at Mount Gabriel indicates that it was in use by 1800 BC. Wooden tools and rock waste from Mount Gabriel have been dated to c.1500 BC. The mines in Ireland which have survived had produced 370 tons of finished copper (estimated from the cubic area of extracted ore and its end-product), more than a hundred times the copper content of all the prehistoric bronze artefacts recovered from the whole of Ireland.

We know that copper and bronze artefacts were being made in Ireland well before the dates from Mount Gabriel. Ireland was also producing large quantities of goldwork at this early date. We know of 81 'lunulae' (crescent-shaped gold sheets which were probably worn suspended from the neck), mostly found in Ireland and south-west England. They were decorated with punched zigzags and hatched triangles, in the same fashion as the Irish axes, such as the one found at Mount Pleasant. Other Irish gold from this period includes pairs of sun discs – small, ornately decorated, circular sheets of gold. A nugget of gold found in Co.

Wicklow had the same composition of trace elements as these artefacts, indicating their likely place of origin in the Wicklow Hills.

The Cornish tin deposits could easily have provided the essential supply of tin for making bronze. Unfortunately there is no evidence that it was extracted in this period though much evidence for early mining has been destroyed by later working. Alternatively the early supplies of tin came all the way from central Europe. Perhaps the presence of Irish gold, in the form of the lunulae, in Cornwall is the only indication that we have of trading contacts between the two areas, which may have involved the extraction of tin and its shipment from Cornwall to Ireland in exchange for Irish produce.

The smelting and casting of copper and bronze require high temperatures. Copper melts at 1083 degrees centigrade (1981°F), a temperature which can be achieved in a small, open bowl furnace with charcoal as fuel. The copper ores, such as malachite and azurite, are broken up and placed in the furnace. The heat is obtained by using bellows to create a strong through draught. The molten metal collects in the bottom of the bowl furnace and cools to form a 'cake'. This 'cake' can be heated again, in crucibles of heat-resistant clay, until it liquifies. It is then poured into moulds of fine pipe-clay or stone or even of bronze. The earliest axes appear to have been cast in single piece moulds but later on artefacts were cast in bivalve or two-piece moulds. No Bronze Age furnaces have been found in Britain but moulds often turn up on settlements like Springfield Lyons or Trethellan Farm (p.116). Although metalworking may seem to us to be a pragmatic industrial process, the ability to turn rock into liquid and then into metal may well have been thought of as awesome and magical. In many societies, smiths are often set apart from the community because of the powerful forces with which they are associated. This may well have been the case in the Bronze Age.

The Beaker people

The use of metal appeared alongside a new style of pottery: finely made and elaborately decorated beakers (75). The Irthlingborough and West Cotton burials were equipped with pots in this very distinctive style, known as

Beaker ware. Beaker pots are generally tall, open-mouthed, narrow-necked vessels with an S-shaped profile. They are covered with intricate, if not fastidious, decoration of impressed cord and incised lines in bands down the sides. They formed a universal pottery style across

75 *The Beaker pot from Green Low, Derbyshire (see also **76**).*

Europe from Norway to Algeria and from Britain to the Danube. They were regularly included in graves, along with a set of items such as arrowheads, wristguards and daggers. Archaeologists have termed these regular associations the Beaker 'package' (**76**). In Britain, beakers were used between *c*.2700 and 1700 BC, a period of over a thousand years. It used to be thought that they were the hallmark of a particular tribe or people, the Beaker folk, who had swept across Europe from the East, bringing knowledge of metalworking with them. They were considered to be a different racial stock from the indigenous farmers of Britain. Their skulls were relatively wide (brachycephalic) whereas those of the natives were narrow (dolichocephalic). More recent studies have pointed out that there was more variation in all skull sizes than previously stated and that, from the time of the long barrows (*c*.4000–3200

BC), to the Beaker burials (*c*.2700–1700 BC), the differences could be accounted for by gradual genetic changes in a single population. So were the beakers brought by migrating people or were they traded, or did local communities just copy the new fashions? People, objects and ideas had been travelling considerable distances across Europe for hundreds of years by this time and the answer is probably a little bit of all three.

The popularity of this pottery style may well have been due to its contents, rather than the pots themselves. One clue comes from an analysis of the pollen grains in a decayed organic layer in a grave at Ashgrove, near Fife in Scotland. The types of vegetation indicated by the pollen were completely out of place in southern Scotland 4000 years ago. There was a lot of lime pollen (linden tree) which did not grow north of Cumbria. On closer analysis, it appeared that the pollen had come from the liquid contents of the beaker, which had spilled all over the organic layer. Lime flowers are precisely what we would expect in an alcoholic honeyed drink such as mead, made from fermented lime honey and flavoured with meadowsweet. Perhaps the secret of the Beaker success was the alcoholic contents of their pottery. It has also been suggested that the cord used to decorate beakers was hemp or cannabis, which was combined with alcohol to produce a strong cocktail. Beakers have been found in the graves of men, women and children but the larger, finer vessels tend to be found in the graves of men (**77**). This may have been the first alcoholic drink; or it may have embodied a change to a new and more personal association with alcohol. Previously, pottery shapes and sizes seem to have been suitable for communal consumption of food and drink. Now, many individuals had their own drinking cup.

We also know that in south-west Britain, the beakers were not traded over long distances but were probably made locally (**78**). Perhaps each individual made their own beaker, with which they were buried. However, many of the items found in graves with beakers did travel considerable distances. Amber beads were carried across Europe from the Baltic. Fine flint tools and weapons were also moved great distances, as far as we are able to tell from identifying their sources of origin. Beaker burials from continental Europe include a few

76 *The grave goods from a round barrow at Green Low, Derbyshire. They include barbed-and-tanged arrowheads, a group of flint tools, two bone spatulae and a bone toggle.*

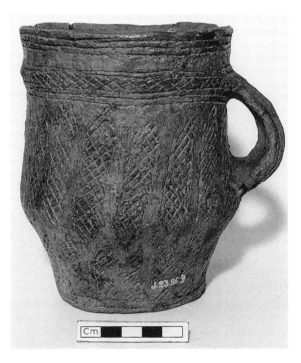

77 *A handled beaker.*

with small stone anvils and tools which were the personal kits of metalworkers. Some archaeologists consider that the people who used beakers brought the secrets of metalworking with them. Metals were certainly being moved at this time: an Irish copper axe has been found in Germany. But the metal trade may have reached Britain before the arrival of the beaker cult; a find of copper axes at Castletown Roche in Ireland included a continental import which probably dates to the time before beakers were first used in the British Isles.

It was also thought that the 'Beaker people' brought with them the art of horseriding. There is no certain evidence for this though the skeleton of a domesticated horse has been found at Newgrange and dated to c.3400–2700 BC. The imprecision of this date prevents us from knowing whether imported, domesticated horses had already arrived in the centuries before the Beaker people. Horse bones have been found in earlier Neolithic contexts at Fussell's Lodge long barrow and Etton causewayed enclosure, and in Late Neolithic contexts at the large henge enclosures like Durrington Walls and at the mines of Grimes Graves. However, we cannot tell whether they were from wild or domestic animals. Whatever the uncertainties of initial origins, the use of beakers was almost certainly linked to the widespread availability of metal, horses and

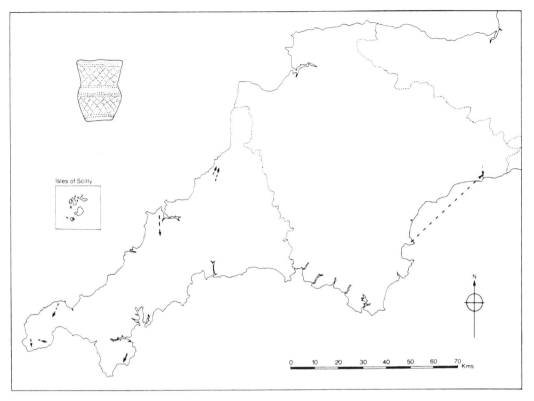

78 *The distribution of Beaker pottery in south-west Britain and its likely (dashed line) or certain (full line) place of manufacture.*

fine equipment. It was a truly cross-continental network which brought together people, ideas and goods across great distances. Britain's links to the continent were primarily to the Rhineland and to the Netherlands.

The adoption of beakers in the British Isles varied from region to region and even within particular regions. They never really caught on in Orkney or south-west Ireland. In Wessex their earliest occurrences were in relatively simple burials and, curiously, in the upper fills of causewayed enclosures and long barrows. These monuments had been long abandoned, for between 500 and 1000 years, and the beaker sherds were found in the tops of ditches which had silted up over centuries of disuse. Beaker sherds were also found in the deposits which were now stuffed into the chambers of the old tombs. The tomb at West Kennet, used for disarticulated burials around 3600 BC, was blocked up with huge stones and its chambers were filled up with chalk rubble, as well as pieces of beakers (**colour plate 10**). This

rubble included layers of rich, dark soil which would have made good fertilizer for the fields. Why waste it on the dead? Unusually, this soil contained pieces of Peterborough Ware and Grooved Ware as well as Beaker Ware, all of which rarely occur together in association at that date. On closer inspection, these deposits proved to be even more mysterious. The Peterborough Ware pottery in this soil had different decorations depending on which chamber it was in. Was each chamber filled by a community from a different area or ancestral line?

The earliest Beaker burials were located at some distance from the great henges, in completely different parts of the country. It seems that the earliest devotees of the Beaker drinking cult were outside the mainstream of society. Why were they involved in activities with the long disused monuments of forgotten ancestors? Perhaps places like West Kennet were being sealed up forever, their sacred power effectively turned off. Alternatively, their filling accompanied a change in their significance: their contents could never be removed. In eastern England, the richer Beaker burials, such as the one from Barnack (Cambridgeshire), are found some miles away from the

79 *The massive timber entrance way to the palisaded enclosure at Mount Pleasant, Dorchester, as it may have looked in the Beaker period.*

earlier cursuses and henges. Perhaps the beaker users were locked in a power struggle with the henge-building 'establishment'.

Beaker sherds have been found in the later phases of the henges, probably left there many years after the timber circles had gone out of use. Some of these abandoned places were re-inhabited by beaker users. At Mount Pleasant (**79**), a large and imposing timber palisade was built within the henge around 2100 BC. It was 800 m (265 ft) long and used 1600 large trees. About 364 ha (900 acres) of oak forest had to be felled for the timber. Inside the palisade the central timber ring of the earlier henge was replaced by a circle of standing stones. It seems that the old centres were taken over by devotees of an increasingly popular Beaker cult. After *c*.2000 BC beakers were still placed with individual burials but the style was more widely used for the storage and cooking wares of daily life. Their specialized role as individual drinking cups had gone and they were now all-purpose containers, used in large quantities in the settlements.

Sacred landscapes of the dead

The use of beakers coincided with a phase of monumentalization in stone. The first stones at Stonehenge (known to us as Phase II) were put up at this time. These were the famous bluestones from the Preseli Mountains in Wales (**80**), which were erected in a circle.

There may have been a timber predecessor on the site but the excavation records are too uncertain on this point. We know that one of the bluestones has a mortice hole in it, indicating that it was intended to be set up as a lintel rather than a standing stone. It, and the other bluestones, might even have been taken from another monument. A long barrow, which went out of use over 500 years before, Boles Barrow (Wiltshire), had a Preseli bluestone built into it. Perhaps the bluestones had arrived in Wessex hundreds of years before they were incorporated into Stonehenge. Around 2000–1800 BC the bluestone circle was abandoned and the large sarsens were put up. These are the huge grey sandstone uprights and lintels that can be seen today.

Recently a group of geologists have come up with evidence that the bluestones were moved from Preseli to Wessex not by people but long before, by an Ice Age glacier. Analysis of the chemical composition of the stones confirms not only their common origin in the Preselis but also identifies different outcrops within the Preselis from which they originated. Why should people have selected bluestones from a variety of different sources rather than one outcrop? The geologists also point to the evidence of the Preseli bluestone in Boles Barrow and the discovery of weathered bluestone cobbles from Stonehenge itself, suggesting that these were glacial erratics. They also found evidence for boulder clearance on Salisbury Plain in recent centuries, which may have resulted in the burial of unwanted bluestone erratics in pits. As a result of these clearances, any bluestones which may have been lying around on the plain, originally dropped by glaciers, have disappeared. Their proposal seemed very convincing but another geologist has pointed out an important anomaly in their argument. If bluestones had been carried to Salisbury Plain by an ice sheet and deposited across the landscape, why had his study of some 53,000 pebbles from stream beds in that area failed to identify a single glacially-derived stone, let alone a bluestone pebble?

Whatever the truth about the movement of the bluestones, they were collected together

80 *Round Bronze Age stone cairns at Foel Trigarn in the Preseli mountains, where the Stonehenge bluestones originated.*

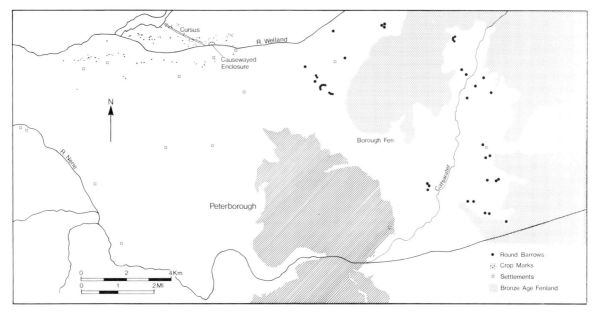

83 *The distribution of Neolithic and Bronze Age settlements and monuments in different areas north of Peterborough.*

and erected at Stonehenge at this time. The Mount Pleasant stone circle and the West Kennet tomb facade and blocking were also erected. At Arbor Low (Derbyshire) large stones were arranged in a ring inside the henge but were never put up (**81**). The stones of Avebury, and its Avenue leading to the Sanctuary (a timber henge with standing stones added) may also have been put up at this time.

Many of the old or ancient earthworks and monuments became focal points in landscapes devoted to the dead. The henges, cursuses, long barrows, stone circles and standing stones attracted cemeteries of round burial mounds, or round barrows (**82**). Over 30,000 round barrows or cairns are known from Britain alone and they were often grouped in numbers of between 4 and 40. Some of these barrows were enormous. The largest are over 50 m (164 ft) in diameter. The Stonehenge barrows number

81 *(Above left) The henge at Arbor Low, Derbyshire, with the standing stones that never stood.*

82 *(Below left) Early Bronze Age round barrows on Normanton Down, south of Stonehenge. Bush Barrow, part of this linear cemetery, is 200 m (656 ft) to the left of this photograph.*

over 260 in a 3 km (2 mile) radius of the stone circle, and are matched by another large barrow group to the east on the other side of the Avon. Smaller groupings were found in Scotland in the Kilmartin valley and on Orkney around the Ring of Brodgar. The Irthlingborough barrows were part of a larger group between two tributaries of the river Nene, clustering around a long barrow at one end and a small cursus, long mound and probable henge at the other. This group was just one of many located along the lighter soils of the eastern river valleys. These sacred landscapes seem to have been spaced every 10 km (6 miles) or so along the valleys, possibly boundaries and meeting places between different territorial groups.

Glimpses of the large-scale organization of the landscape can be gained in these eastern river valleys, thanks to dedicated fieldwalkers (finding flints and other traces of settlements) and intensive aerial photography. In the area north of Peterborough, there seems to have been an area set aside for the burial monuments of the dead (partly focused on an earlier cursus monument) and another zone, further west, where people lived (**83**). Further east in the Snail valley, near Ely in Cambridgeshire, was a 'living landscape', full of settlements yet devoid of funerary monuments. Where the living resided and where the dead reposed might be two completely different regions.

Not everybody was buried under a round

84 *Vegetation marks of ploughed out Bronze Age round barrows at Barrow Hills (Oxfordshire).*

barrow. Flat cemeteries with Beaker burials have been found at Eynsham and Cassington in Oxfordshire. At Barrow Hills, also in Oxfordshire, just south of the Neolithic rectangular barrow, a group of round barrows was built in the same place as an earlier group of flat graves (**84**); it was only because the archaeologists looked at the area between the barrows that the graves were found. They formed a small cemetery with many of the bodies accompanied by beakers (**85**). Only one of the graves had been marked, by a small, causewayed ring ditch. Inside this grave was the crouched skeleton of a man, with a beaker and five barbed-and-tanged arrowheads (a new style of triangular point which replaced the leaf-shaped arrowheads of the Neolithic), possibly in a quiver. An arrowhead jutting from his lower spine had presumably killed him.

While the large funeral monuments and the reused monuments from the past probably gave a reassuring feeling of permanence and perpetuity to the people of the Early Bronze Age, their habitations have been notoriously

difficult to find, no doubt because of their flimsy nature. Only the remains of the past and the dead were fixed into the landscape; by contrast, the communities of the living were fluid and impermanent. Irregular stake-built houses have been recovered from outside the passage grave at Knowth, from under burial mounds at Trelystan in Wales (**86**), from a settlement at Belle Tout in Sussex and from under a Saxon barrow at Sutton Hoo in Suffolk. Each had only survived the last 4000 years because of fortuitous lack of disturbance. These houses were not rectangular, in contrast to some of their Neolithic predecessors. The cattle skulls from Irthlingborough may provide a clue to this transient domesticity. Perhaps cattle herding provided the mainstay of people's lives. The cattle were grazed for most of the year in small herds dispersed across the landscape, coming together in the summer months on the long-established sacred landscapes where the dead were buried. People may have been on the move with the cattle for most of the year within the large territories, so settlements would be impermanent and insubstantial. Perhaps these sacred landscapes brought people together from different territories.

There were undoubtedly conflicts and clashes over territories and herds. A number of burials

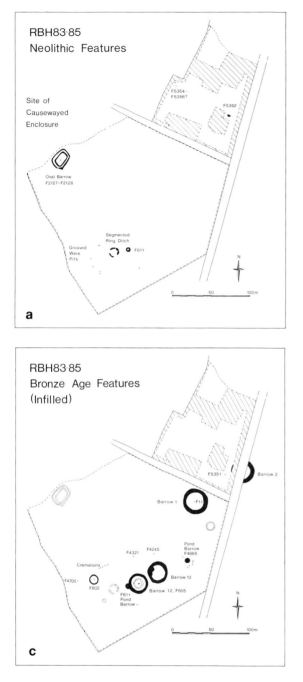

85 a–c *The development of the burial ground at Barrow Hills, in the Neolithic, Beaker and Early Bronze Age periods.*

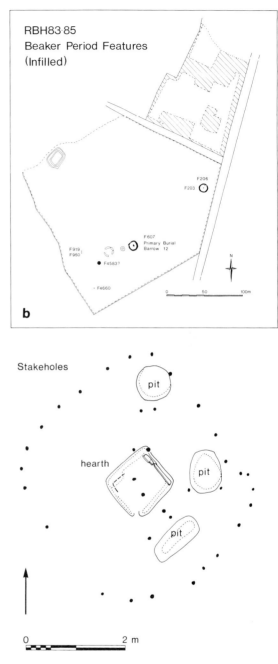

86 *Late Neolithic house found under a round barrow at Trelystan, Wales.*

show traces of violence on the skeletons. A skeleton under a round barrow at Amesbury was missing a right arm while another in the same barrow had its hand severed. A young man, buried in the ditch at Stonehenge, died from arrow wounds. He had been hit by three arrows, in the front and back. The tips of the flint arrowheads had broken off in the bone. Another example of a fatal arrow wound is the burial at Barrow Hills, already mentioned. A substantial number of burials from this period are partly disarticulated. Some bones are displaced and others are missing. This probably resulted from exposure of the dead, possibly on wooden platforms, with the partially rotted corpses then bundled up and buried. It is not unusual in other societies today for the dead to be left unburied for many months while the mourners arrange for elaborate and costly funerals. Finally, a curious feature of this period is the practice of trepanning, the removal of pieces of skull from living individuals. Circular discs of bone had been cut, presumably with a flint implement, from the skulls of two individuals. One of these, buried with a beaker at Crichel Down (Wiltshire), had probably not survived the operation. The bone had not repaired itself and the disc was put back in its hole when the body was buried. The practice is also known from the Neolithic but does not seem to have been particularly common. It may have been a form of either medical or magical treatment, or both.

The Wessex people

A few of the Beaker burials had small gold ornaments, such as 'basket ear-rings' and gold buttons. After 2200 BC more graves were equipped with gold ornaments, notably in southern Britain and especially in the Wessex region. These finds have led some archaeologists to talk of an age of gold in Wessex and they considered that the burials indicate the presence of a new group of people, the Wessex culture. However, the amounts of gold are small and goldwork has been found in only 20 occurrences. The material could fit into a shoebox! The Irish gold, in contrast, is much more plentiful but it was very rarely placed in graves. It has been suggested that all the gold from Wessex of the period 2200–1900 BC may have been made and decorated by one person. The Wessex graves also contained other imported goods which indicate the continental links of a warrior elite.

One of these burials was found in the nineteenth century under Bush Barrow, just to the south-west of Stonehenge. The man buried under Bush Barrow had a beautifully decorated gold lozenge on his chest, and was accompanied by three enormous bronze daggers (one was destroyed in excavation). There was also a stone mace and, apparently separate, a 'baton'

decorated with gold. One of the dagger handles was inlaid with thousands of tiny gold pins. People have suggested that he might have been the architect of Stonehenge when the large sarsen uprights and lintels were erected. However, this is rather fanciful; the grave goods simply happen to be the most elaborate among the Salisbury Plain burials at that time. Others consider that he and the men buried with wealth in other mounds in the south were cattle barons, particularly successful pastoralists who carried their wealth in portable form.

Whatever the answer, these men had considerable cross-Channel connections. Presumably they were powerful and influential local leaders who were able to exchange other forms of wealth for the imports, and whose subsequent exchange contacts would impress their own local communities. The daggers were made of a foreign metal and are identical to those buried in similar graves in Brittany. Gold ornaments crafted in Wessex have also been found in Brittany. There were some similarities in styles with central Europe but the question archaeologists have been asking for years is whether the Greek civilization, centred at Mycenae, had any influence on this area and on the building of Stonehenge. The citadel at Mycenae incorporates monumental masonry in its walls and 'Lion Gate', and archaeologists used to think that this style of architecture was employed at Stonehenge. There is a carving of a dagger, thought to be of Mycenaean style, on one of the large sarsens at Stonehenge. Also an amber disc from Knossos on Crete is bound with gold decorated in Wessex style. There are a handful of Mycenaean bronze axes and swords in Britain but nobody knows if they were really discovered in this country. A fragment of a bronze sword, probably Mycenaean, was found at Harlyn Bay in Cornwall. A gold cup from Rillaton in Cornwall was once thought to be Mycenaean but is far more like the amber, shale, silver and gold cups from Britain, Brittany and Germany. These cups derive their shape from the earlier pottery beakers; those popular pots were later modelled in metal and precious materials. Another supposed link between Wessex and the Aegean was thought to be the tiny blue beads of 'faience' found in graves in Wessex and southern England. About 250 beads of blue faience (an early form of glass) have been found in Britain. For many years, archaeologists thought that these had been made in Egypt but recent tests indicate that they were probably manufactured in these islands.

Some archaeologists once strongly asserted that Stonehenge could not have been built without the influence of Mycenae. When the calibration of radiocarbon dates became possible, it was evident that burials like Bush Barrow and the erection of the sarsen circle at Stonehenge were centuries earlier than the building of Mycenae. But we must not forget that people forged contacts over considerable distances. Europe was criss-crossed by long distance trade routes. Objects could travel a long way along these routes without there being any direct connection between the ends of the routes. An amber bead with gold decoration in the Wessex style has been found in Switzerland, an area which had links to the Aegean. There were links, albeit indirect, with Mycenae but they were likely to have been tenuous. Stonehenge's origins lay in the timber circle tradition and not the stone monuments of the Mediterranean. But Europe was a complex web of networks and not a continent of isolated communities.

6 CAUSES OF CHANGE

In the earlier part of this century, almost all changes in the prehistory of Britain were explained by invaders or migrants coming from abroad and bringing new styles of artefacts, new inventions and new ideologies. The first farmers drove the gatherer-hunters to extinction or integrated them into the farming life. There was then a 'Secondary Neolithic' when the gathering-hunting lifestyle was supposed to have made a comeback (now dismissed since the time length is known to be so great). Then came the invasion of the Beaker people, bringing with them knowledge of alcohol, metal-working and horseriding. Change was considered to have come from outside; it had always happened elsewhere.

The radiocarbon revolution demonstrated that the great tombs of Newgrange and Maes Howe, among others, could not have been built by 'megalithic missionaries' from the Mediterranean. It was still possible for Mycenaeans to have built the last stage at Stonehenge but closer study of the evidence for links with that part of the world showed this to be unlikely. In the years that followed these discoveries there was something of a reaction against the invasion theories, perhaps too strongly in the other direction. Trade was invoked as a central cause of change. Where artefacts could be demonstrated to have moved long distances, these were the result of trade. The exchange of goods was considered to be responsible for the spread of ideas rather than the movements of invaders or migrants. These were societies which did not know money. Goods were presumably bartered or swapped as gifts, each gift entailing an obligation or repayment or service.

Other theories have attributed change to the forces of nature. Some archaeologists see the desertion of the uplands as due to the explosion of Hekla (see p.100). Others blame the weather. It was even suggested that the abandonment of stone circles and astronomical alignments was caused by increasingly cloudy skies as the climate deteriorated. In these days of current concern with global warming, there is perhaps more archaeological interest in how self-inflicted were the various natural disasters and how the human populations coped with the devastating consequences. That is, people are assumed to have had social capabilities which made them more than helpless victims of natural forces.

Others have emphasized internal growth and development. The more that communities became organized into hierarchical and specialized groups the more likely they were to be successful in using the world around them and defeating competitors. The societies which succeeded were those that had hit upon the most effective ways of organizing and co-operating. Their command structures were headed by chiefly families who not only kept the commoners in order but also distributed wealth and protection down through the network.

For yet others, prehistory is an era of struggle between women and men, elders and youth, chiefs and commoners. Society was permanently in conflict, either open or latent. The ruling groups dominated the rest, exacting tribute and labour, and controlling through the ultimate sanction of violence. Social changes came about when the ruling groups, whether male elders or hereditary chiefs, were unable to sustain the premise on which their power lay.

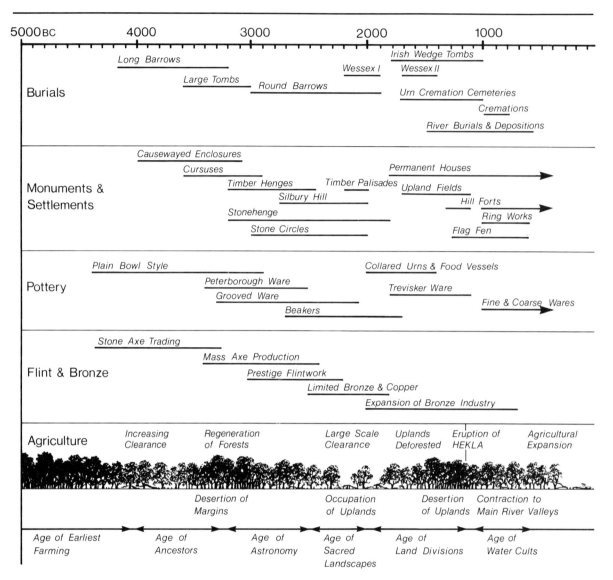

87 *Time chart showing main trends and changes.*

This may have been the chief's failure, as guardian of the crops and animals, to ensure a successful series of harvests; or of elders becoming increasingly powerful but no longer able to hide the fact that the supposedly communal labour projects were enhancing their power rather than that of the community as a whole.

If the complexities of history are anything to go by, then prehistory is a very difficult business indeed. If we can talk about causes then they are likely to be multiple and complicated. Perhaps the only answers to our questions about why things happened are going to be those that derive from our present and not from the past. But the most interesting question is the question 'Why?'. We must continue to ask it.

1 *(Above)* The long barrow at Belas Knap, Gloucestershire. There is a false entrance at the front and access to the interior was by a side passage.

2 *(Left)* West Kennet long barrow.

3 *(Above)* Silbury Hill, the largest artificial mound in Europe.

4 *(Left)* The dimpled landscape of filled-in shafts of flint mines at Grimes Graves, Norfolk.

5 (*Above*) The galleries running off from an excavated shaft at Grimes Graves. The bars and props are modern.

6 (*Below*) Avebury henge.

7 (*Left*) Reconstruction of the building of Avebury henge.

8 (*Below*) The Stones of Stenness, remnants of a circle of twelve standing stones inside a small henge, Orkney.

9 (*Above*) The stone circle at Castlerigg in Cumbria is thought to date from the Late Neolithic or Early Bronze Age.

10 (*Below*) The large sarsen stones erected in the Beaker period to block up the entrance of the West Kennet chambered tomb.

11 (*Above*) The huge Bronze Age stone cairn at Memsie, Banff and Buchan. It is the only survivor of a group of three cairns.

12 (*Below*) Stonehenge in 1990 after some of the stones had been vandalized (the painted letters LIVE are here covered with sacking).

13 *(Above)* A circular Bronze Age kerbed cairn, partially excavated, at Mousland, in Orkney.

14 *(Right)* The stone cist and its contents – cremated human bones – within the kerbed cairn.

15 (*Left*) The hoard of gold ornaments under excavation at Heights of Brae.

16 (*Below*) The Late Bronze Age enclosure and wooden buildings at Springfield Lyons, Essex. The artist has portrayed it as a farming settlement though it may have had a ceremonial purpose.

5

Dividing up the land

Dartmoor has long been known for its impressive Bronze Age monuments. At Merrivale there are stone hut circles and stone alignments. Grimspound is a large stone-walled enclosure with hut circles inside. These are just two of the hundreds of settlements that have survived on the moor since their construction 3500–3000 years ago. In the 1970s Andrew Fleming and John Collis used to take groups of students from Sheffield University on a field study course to Dartmoor. They taught the students to recognize the remains of these deserted settlements and to record and map them. During their surveying, they noticed that the moor was criss-crossed by very slight earthworks which ran in relatively straight lines. On closer inspection these earthworks were found to be low, collapsed walls of stone, covered by turf and heath. They were the remains of field walls which enclosed large rectangular fields and ran for several miles in some cases. These remains had been noticed and written about in the nineteenth century, when they were considered to be medieval field boundaries and were called 'reaves' (88). Parts of the moor had certainly been settled during the medieval period (we can still visit the deserted medieval village of Hound Tor) and people had assumed that these reaves were medieval in date. Fleming and Collis had not only re-discovered a lost knowledge of the reaves, they were also to find out that these field systems were considerably older and more extensive than anyone had realized.

Over the next ten years Andrew Fleming surveyed and recorded the huge network of reaves across the moor and proved that they were set out over three millennia ago. His story is told in his book *The Dartmoor Reaves*. There

had been a human presence on the moor on and off since the last gatherer-hunters and the earliest farmers. The thin tree cover was partially cleared by 4000 BC. There were further clearances around 2500 BC and the moor was almost entirely deforested by 1500 BC. Tiny pockets may have survived, such as the gnarled and stunted trees of Wistman's Wood that can be seen today. Excavations by Andrew Fleming and also by English Heritage's Central Excavation Unit showed that some of the stone reaves were built on top of earlier field boundaries. These were not built of stone and had been laid in segments, one length consisting of wooden posts forming a fence and another length with traces of root disturbance, the remains of a hedgerow. Equally, some of the houses of this earlier phase had been built of timber. Such remains do not show on the surface and can only be found by excavation; we can only guess at their extent. But when the trees had all been cut down, houses and field boundaries had to be constructed out of stone (89). The houses probably had turf roofs while the reaves formed small hedges. The farming communities living on the moor were able to cultivate cereal crops. We can tell this from the presence of cereal pollen and the occurrence of lynchets, where ploughed soil has gradually moved down a slope to accumulate against a field boundary to produce the effect of terracing. The moor was also ideal for raising stock, both cattle and sheep, though we do not know whether this was on a seasonal basis with people bringing their animals on to the moor in the summer months to exploit the higher pasture and perhaps to search for tin ore. No doubt the reality was far more complicated than we realize. People farmed this landscape for over three

88 *Bronze Age stone walls or 'reaves' on Dartmoor.*

hundred years. They cleared the fields of granite stones and boulders, which were incorporated into the reaves and house walls. These stones were also heaped up into small cairns, many of which were used to contain the ashes of their dead.

One of the most unusual aspects of the reaves is their regular layout over many square kilometres. Was this the product of a gradual patchwork of landholdings progressively incorporating more land as fields, as shown by the different segments of fences and hedgerows? Or were the boundaries laid out with considerable planning? The moor was divided by the longest reaves into five main territories and each was sub-divided into large strips formed by parallel reaves (known as 'co-axial field systems'). Some of these strips were further partitioned into smaller fields. There was a central guiding

force at work but what was it? Was there a leader who dictated how the reaves should be laid out? Were there several leaders from different tribes, negotiating for their particular territories? Or were the decisions taken communally among the communities living on and around Dartmoor?

By 1200 BC most settlements and fields on the moor had been deserted. Why had people left? Did they destroy what little fertility there was in the soil? Did the climate become cooler and cause the harvests to fail? Was there some catastrophe in the more fertile lowlands which enabled people to move down from these marginal uplands? Were the upland communities physically moved out and resettled, like the Scottish crofters of the nineteenth century?

The colonization and abandonment of the uplands

Dartmoor was just one area that was intensively settled and exploited. From around 2500

89 *A Bronze Age circular house under excavation on Dartmoor.*

BC large areas of the British Isles were cleared of woodland and opened up for cultivation. There were already sizeable tracts of grassland around the monuments and sacred landscapes on the Wessex chalklands, in the major river valleys of southern England, in the Boyne valley, in Yorkshire, Northumberland and the east of Scotland. The lowlands of Cumbria had been partially cleared but were completely deforested by 1700 BC. The lower slopes of the Pennines were largely cleared by 1800 BC and the upper moors had few trees left by 1200 BC. In Ireland large-scale clearances were initiated after 2500 BC. There were also regions such as northern Scotland where clearance on any scale did not happen until a thousand years later, and there were certainly areas where forest clearance was only partial and where woodland regenerated.

Much of the woodland throughout Britain and Ireland was being opened up and large tracts of upland were settled. As well as Dartmoor, the other uplands of the south-west were divided into field systems. Bodmin Moor and West Penwith have preserved remains from this period. In certain parts of West Penwith, at Zennor for example, the stone walls that were laid out at that time are still in use as field walls and their stumpy remains may be seen underneath more recently built walls. The sands of the New Forest and the Weald were similarly colonized at that time. The limestone uplands of the White Peak in Derbyshire had been settled since *c.*2500 BC but the less fertile soils on the millstone grit of the Dark Peak seem to have been colonized largely after 1800 BC (**90**). The North Yorkshire moors and large areas of western and central Scotland were also settled at that time. In all these regions the shallow and infertile soils could not sustain long-term intensive cultivation and grazing. Something was bound to give at some point. All that was needed was a trigger to accelerate changes already in motion. Archaeologists have argued for years just what that might have been. By 1200 BC many areas of upland began to turn into blanket bogs. In part this was due to the ruinous agricultural practices, but many climatologists think that there was also a gradual deterioration in the weather. The temperature dropped by a couple of degrees and rainfall increased. A second theory is currently being investigated. In 1159 BC a

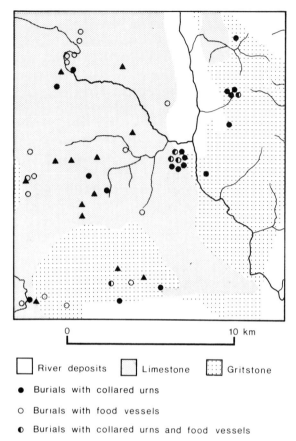

River deposits ☐ Limestone ☐ Gritstone

● Burials with collared urns

○ Burials with food vessels

◑ Burials with collared urns and food vessels

▲ Beaker burials

90 *The distribution of Beaker pots, Food Vessels and Collared Urns in the Peak District of Derbyshire.*

volcano known as Hekla, off the coast of Iceland, erupted with extraordinary force. It sent many millions of tons of dust into the atmosphere. According to some archaeologists, this would have created the Bronze Age equivalent of a nuclear winter. A dense cloud of volcanic ash would have blocked the sun's rays and caused the climate to worsen. The area affected could be identified by a thin layer of volcanic ash which would have settled over northern Britain, with serious consequences for plant life. Harvests would have failed and people in the vulnerable uplands would have been forced to move or starve. Archaeologists have found traces of this volcanic fallout in western and northern Scotland and in Ireland, but recent research suggests that the climate was not radically altered by the eruption. Instead, it

seems that the effect of the volcano was to send huge quantities of sulphur into the atmosphere, which came down as acid rain between 1158 and 1153 BC. Settlements on acid soils were doomed. Not only might the animals have been affected by the discharge, contracting an unpleasant rotting disease known as fluorosis, but the crops would have failed. However, the theory does not explain why the chalk uplands of the south were also deserted around this time. Perhaps many factors, local and far-reaching, were involved in the depopulation of the uplands.

The last of the monuments

Stonehenge took over 800 years to build and rebuild. Its design was altered many times and in the end it was left unfinished. Its final building phase required the equivalent of 1,750,000 hours of labour – say 1000 people working for nearly a year – to select the large sarsen boulders on the Marlborough Downs, shape them, drag them to Stonehenge and erect them as a central group of 5 trilithons (two uprights and a horizontal) and a ring of uprights and lintels. The joinery techniques employed are those of the carpenter. This was a celebration in stone of a timber building tradition. Perhaps its last phases, dating to 1800 BC, were a remembrance of past glories in wood, the timber circles of several hundred years before. Stonehenge in its last phases may have been a monument to previous monuments, remembered only in mythical terms.

Few archaeological monuments have evoked such powerful emotions and so much speculation. There is no doubt that, throughout its period of use and rebuilding, Stonehenge's primary alignment was the midsummer sunrise. It may also have been used to chart the movements of the sun and the moon, even to predict eclipses. Maybe its builders were continuously attempting to link together the solar and lunar cycles. All sorts of theories have been concocted, from underground energy sources to primitive computers. Most archaeologists consider these theories to be bizarre but harmless. With a growing awareness within archaeology that the past should be accessible to everyone, in many senses it really does not matter what meanings people today give to their ancient monuments. Conflicts over power and control in our modern society are sometimes acted out in arguments about the meaning of the past.

The reuse of Neolithic monuments by people in the Bronze Age should not be considered as the passing down of traditions with unaltered meanings. Meaning is very fluid and what people thought of a place or monument when it was created undoubtedly differed from the meaning given to it 500 years later. We know that the solar observations evident in Stonehenge's layout had been known about long before, by the tomb builders of Orkney and the Boyne valley, if not before that. It was thus the zenith of a knowledge made concrete. Stonehenge was never finished; at some point the building programme was abandoned and the power of Wessex declined.

After the golden burials of 2200–1900 BC, there were no elaborate burials for nearly 200 years in Wessex. And then, at around the time of Stonehenge's last construction phases, there occurs a small group of elaborate burials in the Wessex region. Some of the burials under round mounds were equipped with bronze daggers, stone battle-axes, beads of amber and faience and other personal ornaments. The graves were not as spectacular as the first phase of gold burials, known as Wessex I, but

91 *The Collared Urn cremation and bronze dagger, dug into the side of the Irthlingborough mound.*

they indicate that Wessex was still relatively rich and powerful. The provenance and style of the equipment shows that the people of southern Britain had links with Picardy and Normandy in France and perhaps further east to the Rhine and Switzerland. Many of these items were worn out by the time they were buried. Perhaps they were heirlooms, but they also provide clues for the downfall of Wessex.

Wessex was becoming cut-off, beleaguered and impoverished. The new up-and-coming areas were in eastern England, along the Thames, in East Anglia and Lincolnshire. These fertile regions had cornered the supply of metal from the continent and were pioneering a new way of life very different from the astronomy and monument and barrow building of the old traditions.

Sacred landscapes filled with monuments were abandoned or reordered. More work was going into the setting out of field systems across the country than into the building of monuments like Stonehenge. In some ways, the new land allotment was a monument in itself, incorporating and inscribing boundaries and territories into the landscape. The cremated ashes of the dead were still placed in pots and buried under mounds. But increasingly old burial mounds were reused and very few have not revealed any of these secondary burials.

The Irthlingborough barrow was dug into at this time, around 1800 BC, and six cremations were placed in it, one in a pot accompanied by a small bronze dagger (**91**). The pot was of a type that archaeologists call Collared Urns (**92**). These were used as cremation containers all over Britain, from Orkney to Cornwall and the east of Ireland. Archaeologists have put considerable efforts into classifying different types of Bronze Age urn: there are Food Vessels (**93**), Cordoned Urns, Encrusted Urns and Biconical Urns. Less effort has been expended on determining the significance of these differences in shape and style. Pots are not people and few archaeologists would now consider each style to represent a tribe or culture. These pots were used for cooking and storage as well as for holding the ashes of the dead. Certain types of pot, the 'Pygmy Cups', were specifically funerary and may have contained incense. After 2000 BC Food Vessels and Collared Urns were regularly used as grave goods, either as accompaniments to inhumations or as holders of cremated ashes. Beakers were to continue in use for another 300 years. Like beakers some 400 years before, Food Vessels and Collared Urns were initially of ceremonial significance

and then became commonplace utensils. Unlike beakers, they were exclusively British, an island tradition not found on the continent.

Food Vessels were given this fanciful name by early antiquarians. Stylistic elements of their shapes and decoration are reminiscent of the earlier Peterborough Ware, and there may have been some continuity between the two traditions. In Yorkshire, Scotland and Ireland they most often accompanied inhumations; in Wales and north-west England they contained cremations. They were also placed in round barrows, sometimes as the first burial. They are occasionally associated with beakers, but outlasted them by 300 years, going out of fashion by *c*.1400 BC. Collared Urns were used over the same timescale but were used for cremations and are rarely found with Food Vessels. If they were buried in the same barrow as a Food Vessel, Collared Urns were always put in afterwards. Archaeologists used to think that this was because they were of a later date. Or perhaps Collared Urns were used by socially subordinate groups? It is intriguing that the colonizers of the Dark Peak in Derbyshire, with its poor soils on millstone grit, buried their dead in Collared Urns while the people of the White Peak, with more fertile limestone soils, used beakers. Food Vessels were used as burial accompaniments in both areas (see **90**).

The tradition of monumental tombs was dying out. In those instances where burials

93 *A Food Vessel and a Collared Urn, used as containers for cremation ashes. The small pot is known as an 'incense pot'.*

92 *A Collared Urn from the Derbyshire Peak.*

94 *Reconstruction of the Later Bronze Age wedge tomb at Island, Cork.*

were made with new mounds or cairns after *c.*1800 BC, rather than inserted into earlier monuments, these structures were considerably smaller. In south-west Ireland a group of stone monuments, known as wedge tombs, probably date to this period after 2000 BC. These small, capped stone boxes are probably the last of the megaliths in the British Isles. A wedge tomb at Island, Co. Cork, has been dated by radiocarbon to about 1200 BC (**94**). In Cornwall and the Scilly Isles, similar small tombs, called entrance graves (such as the one at Tregiffian), contained pottery dating to around 1500 BC. One of these, Knackyboy Carn on the Isles of Scilly, was filled with 70 pots, all containing cremated human bones. We do not know if these urns were inserted into entrance graves of Neolithic date which had been cleared out for reuse in the Bronze Age, or whether the entrance graves were not built until this time.

Houses and settlements

From an archaeological point of view, the landscape of the dead was replaced by a landscape of the living. Settlements were now the permanent feature while the remains of the dead were no longer at the centre of life. From *c.*1800 BC onwards houses were solid circular structures with floor spaces in excess of 100 sq. m (1076 sq. ft) (**95**). They used to be thought of as wooden 'huts' but when replicas were built, their size and sophistication were finally appreciated. Many young and mature trees had to be felled to build a house and sizeable fields of rushes or turf were required to provide the roof. Their doorways tended to face south, the direction of most light during the day, and some were surrounded by an eavesdrip gully to catch

the rain as it trickled off the thatch or turf roofs. There were probably no windows and no smokeholes. Recent experiments with reconstructions have shown that smokeholes in circular houses create draughts which are likely to send sparks into the thatch and set it alight. The houses were no doubt full of smoke at all times when the hearth was lit.

Round houses were grouped in clusters of between two and ten, forming small rural farms or hamlets. Some were surrounded by ditches and banks, which might even incorporate a palisade. Others had no defences but were either in open space or tucked away in one corner of a field system. On Dartmoor all these variations can be seen within a few hundred metres of each other. An enclosure at Shaugh Moor was recently excavated in advance of china clay extraction. Inside the stone wall

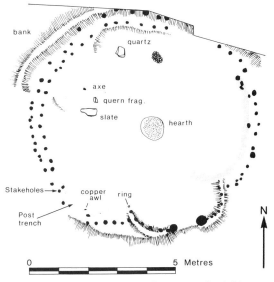

95 *The Early Bronze Age house at Gwithian, Cornwall.*

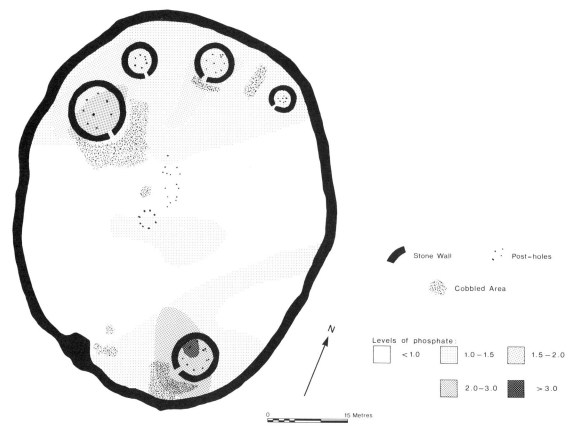

Stone Wall   Post–holes

Cobbled Area

N

Levels of phosphate:

< 1.0	1.0 – 1.5	1.5 – 2.0
2.0 – 3.0	> 3.0	

0   15 Metres

96 *The stone foundations and post-holes of Bronze Age houses and outbuildings within the walled enclosure of Shaugh Moor, Dartmoor. The high phosphate levels show where animals were probably penned.*

were four stone-walled round houses and some possible storage structures. From studies of the phosphate levels and the pottery, the excavators were able to work out that the largest house had been a habitation while the others were outhouses and animal sheds (**96**).

The discovery of loomweights and double post-holes (for vertical warp-weighted looms), spindlewhorls (circular disks for weighting distaffs, used in spinning wool) and combs (for carding wool) in these settlements shows us that textile production was a regular feature of life. Textiles of wool and possibly linen had been in use since at least 2500 BC but it is only from the Middle Bronze Age that the associated tools and technology have survived in abundance. We have some idea of the clothes people were wearing from examples found in exceptionally well-preserved graves in Denmark.

Women were buried in woollen clothes which included long skirts and short tunics. One young woman wore a short skirt of unwoven woollen strands. The men wore knee-length, wrap-around skirts or kilt-like woollens, as well as tunics, cloaks and even one-piece garments. The men were clean-shaven, long haired and wore round woollen hats. Women's coiffure was elaborate; the hair was worn long but held by bands and hair-nets. On their feet, they wore mocassins, sandals and cloth foot-wrappings.

Other activities which archaeology can identify include food preparation and cooking. In some settlements meat was cooked in troughs of water which were heated up by adding fire-heated flints until the water boiled. In Ireland and parts of Britain these boiling troughs have also been found away from settlements. One has been found at Everley Water Meadow, in the valley below Hambledon Hill. They are easily identified by their dumps of heat-cracked stone and are called 'fulachta fiadh' in Ireland. There is some dispute as to whether they were used to cook food; it has been suggested that some were sweat-houses, a

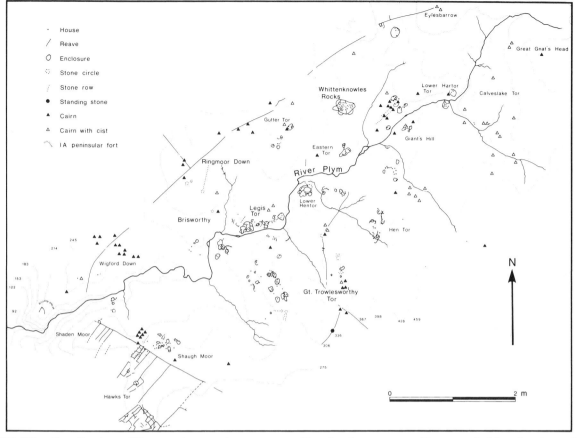

97 *The distribution of Bronze Age settlements, fields and burial cairns in the Plym valley around Shaugh Moor.*

Bronze Age antecedent of the Turkish bath or sauna.

Researchers have found that the standard farming household consisted of two houses: a main living house and a subsidiary house for cooking and other activities like textile production. Perhaps men's and women's activities were segregated. The dead were cremated and their ashes were buried in small cemeteries behind each settlement. Grave goods normally extended to no more than a pot, though a few included the odd dagger or other metal tool.

The large barrow burials of the Early Bronze Age were often strategically positioned where they could be seen from afar and arranged in linear groups. They seem to have emphasized the importance of individuals and their immediate family groups. The dead had dominated the landscape, as they probably dominated people's lives. In contrast, the small cemetery clusters of the Later Bronze Age emphasized the community of the household groups and their attachment to the surrounding land. Perhaps these permanent farms represented a more intensive agriculture focused on arable cultivation. This way of life existed on the more fertile soils in Wessex and eventually ousted the more mobile pastoralist way of life on the chalklands. From southern Britain there are a few of these small settlements that have been excavated. Blackpatch (Sussex), is the most recently excavated and a detailed analysis of the types of pottery and other artefacts, their distribution in and around the houses, and the architectural details of the settlement, has helped us interpret the organization of the community (**98**). The largest, central house was associated with pits for storing grain, fine pottery for eating from, a loom for weaving and a bronze razor (**99**). This has been interpreted as the headman's house. Other buildings are identified as secondary houses concerned with

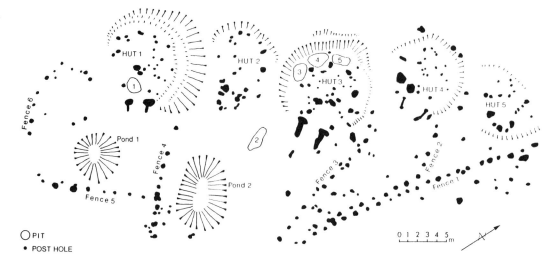

98 *The post-holes at Blackpatch, Sussex – remains of wooden houses and fences which formed a small Later Bronze Age community.*

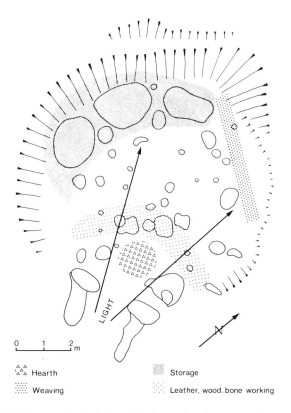

99 *House (Hut) 3 at Blackpatch, showing what activities were carried out in the house.*

food preparation and other domestic tasks, while others may have been outhouses and sheds. The excavator interpreted this community as a large, extended family (**100**).

Similar communities living in round wooden houses (as well as stone ones) are known from Cornwall. At Trethellan Farm, near Newquay, one of these was exposed during construction of a new housing estate. The small cluster of four or more residential houses and several outhouses seems to have formed a little hamlet, perhaps inhabited by two or three families (**101**). In each residential house, people had prepared food and cooked at a central hearth. These round houses were originally divided up by wooden partitions, and there were worn areas of floor where people had slept, knelt or sat (**102**).

In Wessex in the Later Bronze Age the size of settlements corresponds to the extent of the surrounding good agricultural land for each hamlet. By 1300 BC there were four very large settlements in central southern Britain, enclosed by massive defences and located on hilltops. One of these has been partially excavated at Ram's Hill in Berkshire. A heavily defended gateway opened into an interior with many small post-holes and stake-holes which may be the remains of circular houses. These early hillforts may have dominated and controlled larger areas than the smaller groups of farmsteads. They also lay in boundary zones and may have acted as trading centres. The considerable variety of pottery styles found at Ram's Hill matched its unusual location at the

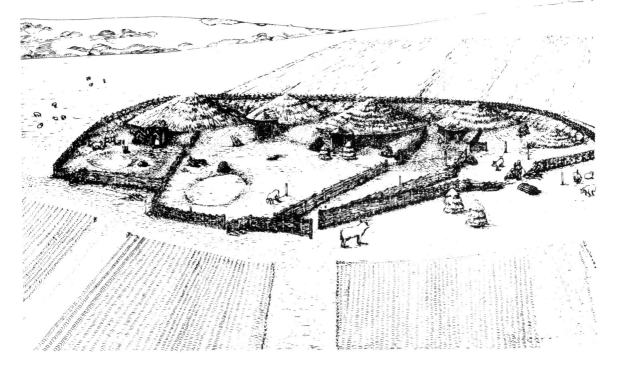

100 *(Above) Reconstruction of the Late Bronze Age settlement at Blackpatch.*

101 *(Below) Trethellan Farm. The Middle Bronze Age settlement as it may have looked.*

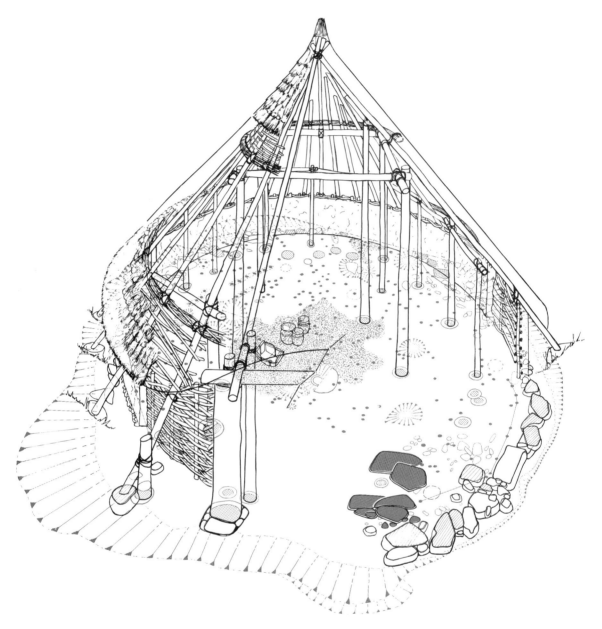

102 *House 2222 at Trethellan Farm. The distribution of stones, post-holes and hearth show what the house would have looked like.*

geographical boundary between different style zones. Some of the finer wares have styles which are geographically distinct. Typically, they cover regions of southern Britain up to 100 km (62 miles) wide. Along such corridors where two or more style zones overlap or coincide the defended settlements like Ram's Hill are found.

Exchange and manufacture

The earlier Bronze Age was characterized by daggers and axes. Daggers were frequent grave goods but axes were only rarely placed with the dead. Axes were most commonly disposed of as single items or in hoards, groups of items that were buried under the ground. The dagger gradually became a pre-eminent symbol. By 1800 BC the people of eastern England were using bronze rapiers, much longer than daggers. These were the forerunners of the

103 Bronze Age pottery of the south-west, known as Trevisker Ware.

the water and must have come from wrecked boats. They were all of continental manufacture. It seems that metal artefacts were crossing the Channel but were melted down soon after arrival and recast in local styles.

There is other evidence for sea travel, including cross-Channel connections. A barrow at Puncknowle (Dorset) included stones that had come from 30 km (19 miles) down the coast. These may have arrived as boat ballast. Pots made on the Lizard peninsula in Cornwall were used as cremation containers in Wessex. Pots from Brittany have been found in burials in Wessex and on the Isle of Wight. Another pot made on the Lizard peninsula ended up in France near Calais. People were sailing along the coasts and occasionally making a long haul which meant losing sight of land.

After 1800 BC styles of pottery became regionalized. The south-west had its own distinctive style, named after the settlement at Trevisker in Cornwall (**103**). Other regions in southern Britain were also defined by stylistic differences. We know that the Trevisker pots were made in just a few locations, principally on the Lizard, but cannot tell whether pots elsewhere in Britain were made in the homestead or were exchanged from production centres. A century or two later, bronze axes (called palstaves) and ornaments were also produced in regional styles. Many of these style zones were to become the tribal areas of the Iron Age, 1500 years later. Presumably what was happening 3500 years ago was that these ethnic identities were created and given material expression in everyday objects. The defended hillforts, like Ram's Hill, were located precisely on the boundaries of the different style zones. Were these frontier areas vulnerable to raiding by different tribal groups? Or were they neutral trade centres where people from different tribes came to exchange goods?

sword. The people of Wessex were still using daggers, but rapiers were being deposited, for one reason or another, in the more fertile regions of the east. Some of these were imports from France and Holland, and a lively trade in metals was developing across the Channel. An axe found on Dartmoor had come all the way from Bohemia in Czechoslovakia. The mixtures of different types of metal in British bronzes indicate that large quantities of bronze were crossing the Channel. Yet, apart from the odd item or hoard, archaeologists have never found great numbers of continental axes, rapiers, spears or tools. Clues to this mystery come from finds made by divers at Salcombe and at Dover. Bronze artefacts were recovered from the seabed. They had not been thrown or fallen into

7 POTTERY MAKING

Pottery is one of the archaeologist's favourite finds. It tells us where prehistoric settlements used to be and also in what period they were occupied. Pottery has been in use since the beginning of the Neolithic in Britain. It was generally poorly made in comparison to ceramics on the continent, possibly because the people of the British Isles relied more on containers of skin and wood. Pottery can also tell

us something about how people stored, prepared and ate their food, as well as about production and exchange.

Most Neolithic and Bronze Age pottery was fired in simple bonfire kilns, built in a tent shape of twigs and sticks and covered with dry leaves. Clay was prepared with a tempering material, such as fragments of flint or rock, to withstand the temperatures of firing and subsequent use in cooking. Grog (crushed lumps of

104 *(Above) Experimental firing of pottery in a bonfire kiln, with the new pots visible in the ashes.*

105 *(Below) Earlier Neolithic pottery from southern Britain.*

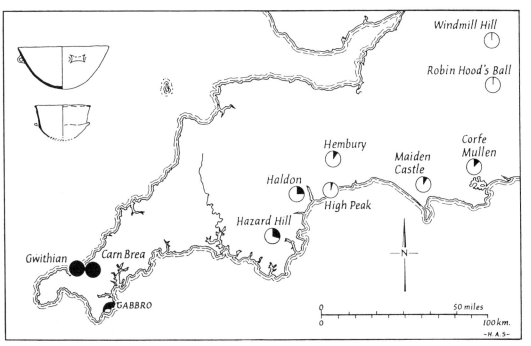

106 *(Above) The distribution of Hembury Ware made on the Lizard. The pie charts show the proportions of Hembury Ware to other types of Neolithic pottery found together.*

107 *(Below) The distribution of Trevisker Ware made on the Lizard.*

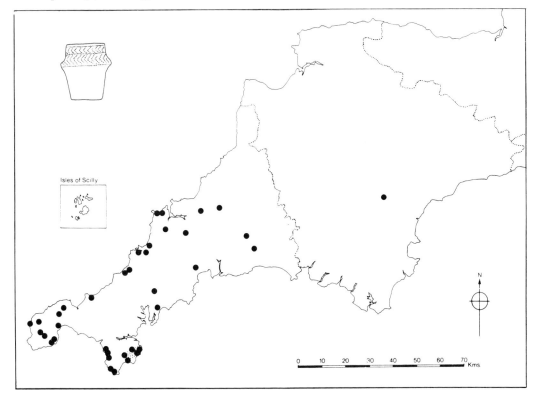

broken pots) was sometimes used as a tempering agent from the Late Neolithic period onwards. The finest Bronze Age pots are the beakers, meticulously decorated, finely made, thin and tempered with fine sand. It was only with the fine wares of the Late Bronze Age, nearly a thousand years later, that pottery of similar quality was made. At that time there were fine wares, probably for eating off, and coarse wares, probably for cooking and food storage.

The Earlier Neolithic pots were round bottomed, presumably for sitting in an ash-bed by the fireside or for cradling in the hand. They were made in a range of shapes and sizes, from small cups or bowls to large jars. Some were relatively fine and others were much coarser. In the Later Neolithic, Peterborough Wares were similarly round-bottomed. Flat-bottomed Grooved Ware also came in a variety of sizes. Beakers were the first individualized pots, made to a relatively standard size and used as accompaniments for the dead. They may have embodied a new attitude towards the individual as an indivisible entity, even in death.

We can recognize standard pottery sizes in the Earlier Bronze Age. Assemblages of pottery from burials and from settlements can be divided into large storage vessels, medium-sized cooking pots and small individualized cups. This is most clearly demonstrated in the material from southern Britain, particularly the south-western pottery style known as Trevisker Ware (see **103**). The division between fine tablewares and coarse storage/cooking wares is noticeable in the globular jars and coarse buckets of the Later Bronze Age, becoming more marked after 900 BC.

It used to be thought that prehistoric pottery was made in the homes in every settlement from local clay. Analysis of the rock inclusions in pottery fabrics has shown that domestic production may not have been that common. Research in south-west Britain (where the rock types are very distinctive) has produced extraordinary findings. In the Earlier Neolithic, relatively finely made bowls with lugs were made on the Lizard. They were made out of a high quality clay known as gabbroic clay; it contains fragments of an igneous rock known as gabbro. Vessels made of this gabbroic clay are known all over Cornwall and Devon but, more surprisingly, they have been found in causewayed enclosures in Wessex, such as Windmill Hill and Maiden Castle. This centralized form of manufacture suggests the presence of specialists making pottery for many different communities, perhaps as gifts exchanged down the line, though some have proposed that they may have been marketed.

We do not know much about the pottery of the Later Neolithic in Devon and Cornwall but it seems that beakers in the south-west were made locally and perhaps domestically. Some were made of gabbroic clay but most were not. Other Early Bronze Age pottery such as Cornish Collared Urns and Food Vessels were predominantly made from Lizard clay. It is especially the Trevisker Ware, in the Early and Middle Bronze Age, which was made on the Lizard. Some of this pottery included fragments of other rocks such as serpentine, which also occurs there. The pottery was transported in bulk throughout Cornwall. All the pottery (weighing nearly 80 kg (176 lb)) from the settlement at Trethellan Farm, on the north coast of Cornwall, had been made 40 km (25 miles) away on the Lizard. Trevisker Ware in Devon was largely made of clays from around Dartmoor but some Lizard products reached here and further afield, as far as Wessex and France. Around 900 BC the pattern of production changed and other clay sources were used in the region.

6

Gifts to the gods

The Fenlands of eastern England were a complex landscape of waterland environments in the Bronze Age. There were areas of open water, of islands and freshwater marsh, and extensive tracts of saltmarsh. Large areas inland from the Wash were underwater. During the Bronze Age thick deposits of peat formed across this wet landscape, burying many of the Neolithic and Bronze Age sites. As a result the peat has protected some of the best preserved remains of British prehistory. Wooden and other organic materials have survived in the wet peat until now. A large-scale project over the last seven years, involving archaeological teams from four different counties, has found over 2000 new archaeological sites. The camps of gatherer-hunters, the monuments of early farmers and Bronze Age burial mounds are all coming to light.

For centuries people have found bronze weapons and tools on the fen margins. Today even more are found by metal detectors. Unfortunately we know all too little about the circumstances under which these items ended up there. Were they lost? Were they hidden and never reclaimed? Were they thrown away because they were no longer of use? Or were they deliberately deposited as offerings to unknown gods and spirits?

These Fenlands have been drained since the seventeenth century. Vast expanses of saltwater marsh and freshwater fen are now some of the most productive arable areas in Europe. But there is a price to pay. As the peat has dried out so it has shrunk and blown away (108). If present agricultural practices continue, the peat will have disappeared in the next century. It took 3000 years to form and has buried archaeological remains which have

stayed waterlogged until now. While we are finding many new sites, the chances of wood and other organic materials surviving are growing slimmer. Also as the plough bites deeper, so it destroys archaeological sites which have lain untouched since their abandonment.

Francis Pryor has been working in the Fens for over twenty years and has carried out major archaeological excavations at Fengate, near Peterborough. Some years ago he discovered massive timber piles buried beneath the peat at Flag Fen (109). They had been exposed when a drainage dyke was cleared out. Excavations revealed that there was a huge platform of worked timbers in what had been the middle of a bay in an inland sea. Dendrochronology has provided dates for Flag Fen of 1365 to 967 BC, with a concentration in the last 150 years of this span. During excavations, which are still continuing, pottery and bronze artefacts were found on the platform.

In 1988 plans for a power station within a kilometre of Flag Fen were well advanced. Trial excavations on its intended site led to an extraordinary find. Rows of timber piles, rapidly drying out and rotting, led from the fen edge into the peat, heading straight for the platform at Flag Fen. We now know that this alignment of timbers stretched for just over 1 km (0.6 miles) from what had been the edge of dry ground at Fengate to Whittlesey, previously an island. Over 2 million trees had been felled, brought to the site, split into radial planks and driven into the seabed. Other timbers were laid on the ground to form a wooden mat or trackway which would have been submerged in winter and exposed in summer. The whole enterprise was an extraordinary undertaking. The timber no doubt came from some

108 *(Above) Two of the Holme Fen posts. Their tops indicate the height of the peat around 1850, showing how much has been lost due to drainage and farming activities.*

109 *(Below) The timber platform at Flag Fen.*

considerable distance away; the Fengate area had been settled since the Early Neolithic by the earliest farmers and was largely open ground by this time. The driving in of the piles was also no mean achievement without cranes or piledrivers.

In the middle of the bay, where the water had been deepest, was the platform. Here there were many more rows of piles and several layers of timber forming a rough surface. Some of the timbers had been reused from demolished houses. It was initially thought that there had been longhouses built on the platform, and that the platform was a settlement, protected by water and accessible only by boat or along the causeway. A recent analysis has revealed types of beetle which are only found in very wet environments. It now seems that conditions were too wet for habitation, and that the timber posts were pilings rather than house uprights. The purpose of the timber alignment is uncertain. The trackway would have been submerged in winter and muddy in summer. A clue to its use was found on the dry land. A few hundred years before, around 1600–1200 BC, there had been a droveway

110 *A broken bronze sword and other artefacts deposited by the side of the Flag Fen timber structure.*

which led into the water at that point. The line of this droveway had been in existence for over a thousand years and was first established by users of Grooved Ware over 4000 years ago. The timbers of the later trackway were almost on the same east-west alignment and seemed to represent a repositioning of the drovers' route where it entered the water. Perhaps the timber alignment was to enable cattle to cross to the pastures of Whittlesey island. But presumably the animals had swum across before so why go to all the trouble of building such a huge structure? It was not a causeway with a platform above the water. The horizontal timbers were pegged into the mud under the water of the bay. The timbers formed an impenetrable thicket which no boat could have sailed through. Was the crossing also a barrier, restricting water traffic from entering the bay? The most extraordinary discoveries were then made in and around the piles on the western, Fengate side. Hundreds of bronze artefacts – ornaments, swords, spears, tools – and animal bones were found (**110**). Helped by local enthusiasts with metal detectors, Francis Pryor's team excavated and recorded each find. They discovered that most of the bronzes had been deposited to the south of the timbers and had probably been thrown from the routeway. One bronze sword was entirely unused and had

never even been sharpened. All the other swords had been broken in half or bent. Similar treatment was meted out to the knives and spearheads. Many of the ornaments had also been smashed and the haft of an axe had been snapped in two. Not all were broken. A unique pair of bronze shears was recovered, still in its carefully crafted wooden box.

What had been going on here? Some of the artefacts were centuries older than the timbers and others were centuries younger. Were they accidentally dropped as people waded through the water? But far too many had been deliberately broken. Were they thrown away because they were already broken? Again, the way that they were broken was not from misuse or accident but quite deliberate. Many of the swords were snapped or bent in the middle in the way in which a disgraced army officer's sword might be broken by his commanding officer in recent centuries. It seems that people had been coming here for centuries to mark the line, before and after the timbers were put up, by destroying and throwing away these valuable artefacts. This was a 'wishing well' on a very grand scale. Recent studies have shown that all around the Fens hundreds of bronze weapons were deliberately thrown away into water, from where they could never be retrieved. The Fengate/Flag Fen structure was just a more focused location for this practice. There is evidence of similar timber structures in other parts of Britain. Flag Fen may help us to make sense of a discovery made over 50 years ago at Clifton, in the river Trent. During dredging operations, some logboats and quantities of bronze spearheads, rapiers and swords were found in an area of wooden piling. The weapons can be dated to c.1100 BC. One day we may know considerably more about these practices.

The makers of bronze

Archaeologists in Essex recently discovered from the air the traces of a huge circular ditch at Springfield Lyons, near Chelmsford. They thought it might be a henge monument but when they excavated it, they discovered that it dated to c.900 BC. At its centre was a round house and around the inside of the ditch was a timber and earth rampart. The two main entrance ways faced east and west. In the ends of the ditches on the north side of the two entrances were two deposits of clay moulds.

These are still being analysed at the British Museum but some have been identified as moulds for casting swords. Despite very careful excavation, not a trace of bronze or other bronze-working debris was found in the interior of the enclosure. Why were there sword moulds at the entrances? Perhaps the freshly cast weapons had been brought there while still in their clay moulds and the moulds broken to reveal the new swords, which were handed over to the people in the enclosure. Or were the ditches simply convenient places to dump the debris of sword making, which had been carried out in the vicinity?

Other moulds for swords have been found in Britain, generally in rather out-of-the-way places like Dainton in Devon and Jarlshof in Shetland. Interestingly, most of the swords ended up in regions at some distance from where there is evidence of their manufacture. The same is true of some tools. There is a distinctive type of axe, known as South Welsh axes after the area where they are principally found. Moulds for making these South Welsh axes have been discovered – but not in Wales, only in southern England. There were considerable connections across the North Sea and the Channel in metalwork styles. Certain types of swords and spears were identical on either side of the Channel. Many aspects of south-eastern English material culture had more in common with north-west France than with the rest of the British Isles. New techniques were flooding in. The casting of large objects like swords required considerably greater skill than casting axes or daggers. Sheet-bronze working also developed to new levels: bronze cauldrons and shields now appeared on the scene. The 'lost wax' process was also developed and objects such as crotals were made by Irish smiths. These were hollow cast balls which contained a bronze 'pea' and it has been suggested that they were representations of a bull's scrotum and were perhaps connected with fertility. Bronze smiths also began adding lead to the bronze. This certainly made the metal go further but rendered it softer. By c.700 BC large numbers of axes had such a high lead content that they would have been of no use in cutting down trees. Archaeologists have suggested that some symbolic use had overtaken the practical purpose of an axe and that bronzes were increasingly a form of currency to exchange for other goods.

Goldworking also reached new heights. Collars, neckrings, bracelets, dress fasteners and chestplates were made in gold. Perhaps the most impressive goldworking went into the manufacture of 'lock-rings'. These may have been worn in the hair and were made of tiny gold wires only 0.33 mm in diameter. Most of this gold has been recovered from Ireland, but has also been found in East Anglia and Scotland. Curiously the sources of the ore used are in central and eastern Europe. Perhaps the deposits of gold in the Wicklow mountains were largely exhausted by now.

Thousands of hoards of bronzes and some gold hoards have been found in the British Isles. Some of them consist of only a handful of objects. Others include thousands of pieces and must have been brought in several loads to the place of deposition. Some were buried together in a box or a bag and others were scattered across a wide area. The largest gold hoard of the period was found in 1854 during the construction of a railway at Mooghaun North in West Clare. Over 146 gold objects had been buried in a stone cairn or stone heap. A smaller gold hoard of 11 pieces was recently found in a ploughed field at the Heights of Brae, near Dingwall in Scotland (**colour plate 15**). Four of them were found in a group together and the rest had been scattered around by the action of the plough.

For over a hundred years, archaeologists have divided hoards into a variety of types. Those that contained ingots, scrap and broken metal were called founders' hoards (collected ready for the bronzeworker's foundry). Collections of unused, new weapons or tools were considered to be merchants' or craftsmen's hoards. Groups of ornaments, tools and weapons were considered personal hoards. It was thought that the reason that they had been left in the ground was that their owners had buried them for safekeeping and either had never returned or had forgotten where they were hidden. Rivers like the Thames and the Witham have produced large numbers of bronze weapons from dredging. In the Thames, most of these have been found around Syon Reach and Richmond. It was generally considered that they had been lost by Bronze Age warriors attempting to cross these watercourses. But as one archaeologist has asked, can we really explain all these hoards and finds as due to the incompetence of so many boatmen

and the forgetfulness of so many smiths?

We have very few burials from this period. The practice of cremation continued, but after 1000 BC the ashes tended to be deposited in shallow pits without even a pot as container. By c.800 BC cremation burial rites had virtually disappeared. After that we know very little about the disposal of the dead. There were a few distinctive inhumations with metalwork (such as Handley Cross in Sussex), which seem to be more akin to burials in France. Some of the metal hoards also contain human bone. Many human skulls have been recovered over the years from the same stretch of the Thames where the weapons have been recovered. They were recently dated by radiocarbon and the vast majority were found to date from the same period as the weapons. Were these the remains of defeated warriors whose corpses and weaponry were thrown into the river after a series of riverside battles? Or was this a sacred place where the dead were tipped into the river, along with their personal property? Perhaps the water deposits were part of the funerary rites and west London was at that time a prehistoric version of Benares in India, where the dead were brought for disposal. A closer look at the so-called founders' hoards revealed that they shared a common structure. Far from being random collections of scrap metal, they regularly included particular items: fragments of swords, spears and axes. Perhaps these were also offerings of personal equipment and possessions.

What was the point of throwing away so much wealth? Many suggestions have been put forward. Sacrifices had to be made to the forces of earth and water. By giving things away, people increased their sanctity, honour and prestige. People's standing in the community rested on how much they could give away rather than how much they could accumulate. The destruction of bronzes has also been interpreted as a way of removing them from circulation to prevent their loss of value, a kind of anti-inflationary measure. The most powerful groups could limit the items in circulation so that they did not fall into other people's hands. Finally, these objects may have been gifts which cemented relationships between people (at marriages and funerals for example). When the relationship came to an end – when one person died or decided to end it – the objects were destroyed.

Warfare

The European Bronze Age was perhaps the first arms race. Between 1800 and 800 BC bronze weapons became more and more elaborate. Daggers evolved into rapiers and towards the end of the Bronze Age, the rapier, a thrusting weapon, was replaced by the sword, with its heavy blade more suited to slashing at the enemy. Spearheads also developed over this period and were used for throwing as javelins or for hand-to-hand fighting. From weapon deposits across the British Isles, we can identify three regional traditions of fighting. From Yorkshire to Scotland it was the swordsman that was celebrated in the hoards. In south-east Britain, swords and spears occurred together. In a band stretching from the south-west to the Thames, to Wales and south Yorkshire, weapon hoards were characterized by spears. Some of these spears were broad-bladed and have been erroneously called 'fish spears'. There is some doubt whether they were truly effective weapons.

In 1981 a scuba diver found a bronze shield on the bed of the river Shannon. This was the eighth bronze shield to be found in Ireland. None of them would have been any good in combat. Experiments on replicas have demonstrated that they could not withstand a single sword cut. They were made for show and not for use. Instead, shields of leather and of wood, also found in Ireland, were far more suited to the rigours of battle. Strangely, there are very few arrowheads known from this period. Crude flint tools were still being made but the beautiful barbed-and-tanged arrowheads of an earlier millennium had gone out of use. A handful of bronze arrowheads are known but swords, spears and shields seem to have been the preferred weapons. From European finds, we know that Bronze Age warriors dressed up in bronze helmets, cuirasses and guards for the arms and legs. As with the shields this armour was not designed for active combat. Presumably warriors wore stout leather equivalents when actually in battle. These new kinds of weapons and body armour indicate that all over Europe warfare was waged in a new way. The Beaker archers had been replaced by heavily-armed horsemen and foot soldiers who fought at close range. Archaeologists have suggested that the style of fighting described in Homer's *Iliad* was also employed in western Europe. Warrior elites challenged each other, singly or

corporately, to armed combat. They also raided enemy territory for cattle and treasure.

Some of the few skeletons found from this period indicate the grisly fates occasionally awaiting these warlike people. Around 1000 BC at Tormarton in Somerset two young men were repeatedly stabbed with spears. One had a spear injury in his pelvis, inflicted either from the side or as he was falling. The second had been speared through his spinal cord and through his pelvis. The spears were thrust so firmly into the bone that the killers were unable to pull out the spearheads, which snapped off in the victim's backbone and pelvis. Another unfortunate, found near Dorchester-on-Thames, had also been stabbed in the pelvis and the spearpoint had again snapped off. Since we have so few intact skeletons from the period, it is not possible to know what percentage of the population met violent deaths.

Other indications of a martial and warring society come from the fortified enclosures of the period. Defended hillforts had appeared earlier at sites like Ram's Hill in Berkshire, and in other regions people were similarly defending themselves and their farmsteads. The Breiddin and Ffridd Faldwyn in the Welsh Marches were fortified at this time. A large community, living in some 200 small huts, inhabited the exposed and inaccessible summit of Mam Tor (Derbyshire) (**111**). At Grimthorpe (Yorkshire), a small oval palisaded hillfort was constructed by 1000 BC. Traprain Law, south of Edinburgh, and Beeston Castle were hilltop sites where metalworking was going on and they may also have been defended. Not everyone, though, was on the defensive and we now know of many lowland settlements that had no ditches and banks around them.

Life in the settlements

Since *c*.1300 BC agricultural areas had contracted in size. The more extensive farming practices of earlier centuries had proved unsuccessful in the uplands in particular. The new organization of farming practices was more intensive with a wider range of crops grown. Sites like Springfield Lyons (Essex) were using crops and fodder from a variety of ecological zones. The plant debris from the site tells us that grasses from the water meadows down by the river were mixed up with crops and weeds from the heavier soils in the vicinity. Farmers were attempting to cultivate the wetter and

111 *The Late Bronze Age hillfort on top of Mam Tor (Derbyshire). The dimples are terraces for small huts.*

heavier clay soils which they had largely avoided (apart from woodland management and hunting) since the beginning of farming. On these different soils they grew a wide range of cereals and legumes. There were many more weeds of cultivation; presumably species migrated between plots as land was opened up and as seed corn was moved around. Whereas cattle had been the pre-eminent meat provider since the first farmers two to three thousand years before, sheep were now raised in greater proportions than previously. Fewer pigs were bred, possibly either related to the continuing loss of forest (pigs being good forest browsers), or due to changing dietary fashions.

In Ireland there was a renewal of forest clearance and a rise in farming activity after 1200 BC and a second agricultural upsurge around 700 BC. By 900 BC the last forests in the Upper Thames valley had disappeared. Parts of the Thames valley were also over-exploited, leaving large tracts empty of settlements in the following centuries. An agricultural revolution was taking place which was to initiate a farming economy that continued until the late Iron Age, 600 years later.

Until a few years ago, settlements of the Late Bronze Age were virtually unknown in the British Isles. They are still remarkably difficult to find; they leave few tell-tale signs on the surface since flint tools were hardly used and the coarse but fragile pottery is easily destroyed by the plough. Where they have been found, they conform to a pattern of habitation on the higher and drier sides of valleys, where they tend not to be amenable to discovery by aerial photography. Proposals for a modern graveyard extension on the slope of a river valley at Potterne (Wiltshire) led to the discovery of one of these settlements. A gold bracelet was found in a Late Bronze Age rubbish heap. Underneath this midden were the remains of post-holes and features from an earlier phase of buildings. Only a small proportion of this large open settlement was examined but there was one startling conclusion. The midden was huge, containing thousands of tons of horse dung! Why had it accumulated without being spread over the fields and why did they have so many horses? As we have seen with rubbish in the Neolithic, there may well have been some symbolic aspect, concerned with fertility, to what we see as a giant heap of manure. Potterne was one of many large open settlements which survive in Wessex. At Runnymede, on an island in the Thames, there was a large riverside settlement with rectangular as well as round houses. The copious evidence for working of textiles, bronze and antler, the exotic trade items and the remains of feasting made it clear to the excavators that this was no ordinary settlement. Was it a chief's stronghold or a neutral trading point?

The Thames was no doubt a major waterway for trade and communication as well as an important and sacred river for making offerings. At Wallingford (Oxfordshire) a riverside settlement similar to Runnymede has been discovered. At Marshall's Hill, near Reading, there was a settlement which produced finds similar to those from Potterne, perhaps signifying a chief's residence. In the adjacent stretch of the Thames large quantities of bronze metalwork have been recovered. There were other settlements nearby, and eight of them have been found underneath the Reading Business Park. The most extensively excavated, at Small Mead Farm, seems to have been reliant on pastoralism. The system of paddocks and the water-holes suggests stock management, and the inhabitants seem to have grown flax rather than grain. Perhaps the inhabitants of this and the other settlements were subjects of the people who lived in the large site on Marshall's Hill.

In Essex, a few small open settlements are known but the most interesting sites from this period are the enclosures. We do not know whether Springfield Lyons was a ceremonial enclosure or a domestic residence or, indeed, both. If it was a residence then it was probably more than an ordinary farmstead. The ditch was 2 m (6½ ft) deep and the eastern gateway was of monumental proportions. The visitor, on entering the enclosure, looked straight into the

112 *Pots of the Late Bronze Age.*

porch of the round house in the middle. The front of the compound was kept clean while a group of at least three small structures in the south-west corner were concerned with the activities of food storage, cooking and rubbish disposal. From careful analysis of the charred remains of plants, we know that grain was winnowed in this corner. There were also lots of large fragments from broken cooking and storage pots (**colour plate 16**).

There are always artefacts that baffle archaeologists. One of these is the 'perforated clay slab', a flat slab of lightly fired clay with round finger-width holes in it. They are never found whole and seem to have broken very easily. Archaeologists have suggested that they were used in manufacturing salt or as plates in simple ovens. I favour the latter interpretation since they have been found around the cooking areas at Springfield and at Loft's Farm, also in Essex. Another novel feature from Springfield is the presence of finely-made pottery jars and cups (**112**). These delicate, thin, shiny vessels are the first pottery 'tableware' since the beakers, a thousand years before. Many broken fragments had ended up on the midden by the cooking area but other pieces were found inside the large house. The front of this central house had been kept swept but at the back were shallow scoops which contained freshly broken pieces of tableware. It seems that food was served in this central house, while the preparation took place out the back in the corner of the enclosure. Who was cooking and who was serving? Unfortunately we do not know but there is one clue. The decorations of incised lines and chevrons on the tableware are found on spear-

113 *Reconstruction of the Late Bronze Age settlement enclosure at Lofts Farm (Essex).*

heads in Britain. Perhaps we can guess who was eating from this fine pottery: it looks as though these were symbols of manhood.

At Loft's Farm a smaller rectangular enclosure has been excavated (**113**). It also had a central round house and a cooking area in the southern part of the enclosure. On a gravel promontory overlooking the Thames at Mucking (Gray's Thurrock), were two more circular enclosures. The earliest had two large ditches surrounding a single central round house. Clay moulds indicated that weapons had been made in its vicinity. The later enclosure (dated by its pottery styles) was smaller. Inside the entrance was an enormous timber screen which hid a group of round houses from view. A footpath led from the entrance to an access in the middle of the timber screen (**114**). All these enclosures were well placed to watch over river transport up and down the Thames estuary and its tributaries. Both sides of the estuary were important. Metal supplies were no doubt arriving from the continent and being turned into

weapons and tools. Cattle grazed on the extensive salt marshes and these areas were producing salt. Seawater was trapped in large troughs and boiled until only the salt crystals remained. We know this was happening at Walton-on-the-Naze around 1100 BC.

There was something of a revolution in cooking in the Late Bronze Age. We take salt for granted nowadays, but it must have been an exciting flavourer at that time. It was also a useful preservative for meat. Salt was being mined in the Alps in the Later Bronze Age, but mining may have begun in the Early Bronze Age. In the nineteenth century two Bronze Age miners were found perfectly preserved in one of these salt mines but unfortunately their bodies were buried in a churchyard by the locals. The large bronze cauldrons, found in bogs and in other special deposits, were no doubt used for boiling meat in large quantities. We also find flesh-hooks, long bronze prongs that were used to fish out the meat from the cauldrons. Boiling troughs had appeared earlier. At Rathgall in Ireland another circular stockaded enclosure with central round house had trough hearths for cooking. A gold ring and moulds for

114 *Reconstruction of the Later Bronze Age enclosure at Mucking, north ring.*

weapons were also found there.

In Yorkshire a huge circular enclosure has been excavated at Thwing. It may have once been a henge which was reused around 1500 BC. Its last phase dates to the Late Bronze Age. The large quantities of cattle and pig bones from a rubbish deposit in one of the filled-in ditches show that this imposing site was used for feasting. A final example comes from Ireland at Navan Fort (**115**). In its earliest phase, around 700 BC, a stockaded enclosure was positioned next to a round house. Nearby was an artificial pool from which were recovered sword moulds and human skull fragments. The most remarkable find was a Barbary ape's skull which had come, either live or dead, from Spain. However, this find probably dates to the Iron Age phase of that enclosure's occupation.

All these extraordinary enclosures shared a number of common features. They incorporated the ceremonial and the secular, the industrial and the domestic. They were laid out with some geometrical precision. They were associated with metalworking. Their entrances and the entrances of the round buildings inside them all faced east (rather than south as the earlier houses had done). It is just possible that these were the first constructions put up by Celtic

115 *Reconstruction of a ceremony at the Late Bronze Age enclosure at Navan (Co. Armagh).*

peoples, arriving in Britain around 900 BC. Even today in Gaelic the word for 'west', 'iar', is the same as for 'back'. Likewise, 'tuath' means 'north' and 'left', while 'deas' means 'south' and 'right'. Throughout the British Iron Age and into the Roman period, for the next thousand years, the significant east-facing doorway and entranceway were to be found in the vast majority of enclosures and houses. As people arose in the morning, they left the house facing the sun. When they returned in the evening they continued to face the sun as it set in the west. The practical and domestic chores of everyday life were set within a world of ritual and observance connected with the sun's path.

The end of the Bronze Age

All of these features were as much elements of a new beginning as of an ending. The change from bronze to iron was technological. New resources and new ways of exploiting it were required. Yet this technological revolution seems to have had little immediate effect on the society at large. Earlier archaeologists thought that this was a definitive break in prehistory, when iron users invaded and defeated bronze users. We now know that the adoption of iron began in the 'Bronze Age', probably by 1000 BC in Britain. Iron tools were used in bronze-working from this date and by the end of the 'Bronze Age' iron was being deposited as votive offerings, such as the mixed bronze and iron hoard from Llyn Fawr in Wales. As with the first copper tools, iron was initially inferior to bronze. The earliest iron tools, forged and not cast, were attempts at copies of cast bronze tools, such as socketed axes. The tradition of how tools should be made overruled the most practical shapes that iron tools could be forged into.

From its initial experimental adoption in the Near East, over a thousand years before, iron had been a precious curiosity. Its manufacture into tools and swords required very different resources from bronze-working. Whereas powerful chiefs could control the circulation of copper and tin across distant trade networks, and hence control the manufacture of weapons and tools, iron could be obtained from many different sources. Its manufacture thus had the capability to subvert the power of the bronze-controlling establishment. Iron was potentially a destabilizing force. Its ore was widely available and anyone with the know-how could make iron tools. Yet a crisis in bronze making seems to have arisen in western Europe before iron came properly to dominate the metal industry. By 700 BC the high lead content in bronze axes rendered them ineffective as tools. Britain was flooded by large quantities of these useless axes from Brittany. The metal economy may have been hit by a crisis of overproduction. Perhaps the reason that iron became more widely used was that supplies of bronze were increasingly unpredictable, both in metal content and in general availability. Alternatively, the secrets of the new metal were being traded across Europe. Everybody wanted this innovation and as a result the bottom dropped out of the bronze trade. As the value of bronze axes fell so the addition of lead to increase stocks became viable. They were in any case items of exchange rather than tools for practical use. The Iron Age did not start overnight; nor did the manufacture of bronze artefacts stop. The transition was much more gradual, over half a millennium, starting with a few prestigious iron items, spreading to weapons and tools for working bronze, later on to ordinary tools, and finally to ornaments.

7

The long view

It is never easy to sum up a prehistoric sequence of over 4000 years. During those millennia, over 150 generations of people lived and died, none of them known to us by name but leaving their graves, their houses and their goods for us to identify them. Archaeology works well at two levels of analysis: firstly the sharp focus of detail in recovering those moments when the tomb was sealed or when the rubbish was thrown on the midden; and secondly the blurred outlines of long-term change beyond the lifetimes, and comprehensions, of the people who lived all those millennia ago. People had some control over their personal destinies but their lives and actions were always constrained by the traditions of the past which was continually evoked in the present. To our eyes, their world changed slowly. There were periods of hundreds of years when the material trappings of life evolved hardly at all. There were also times of upheaval, but the archaeologist is often unable to say whether these upheavals happened within one, ten or two hundred years.

Long-term trends in British prehistory

We can isolate a number of trends over these 4000 years. The axe was replaced as a key symbol, first by the dagger and finally by the sword. It is interesting to note that the sword is still a prominent symbol in military display today. The tombs of the dead were replaced by the houses of the living as the most permanent features in the landscape. Again, we take for granted the central importance of the house in modern society. The use of alcohol and perhaps other drugs as ceremonial intoxicants probably originated in this time, with the Beaker tradition, if not before. The landscape was increas-

ingly partitioned into land parcels and territories. A concern with peopling the land was replaced by a concern with dividing it up. People were replaced by land as the most important resource to be controlled. There were also shifts in regional power and wealth. Areas like Wessex were overtaken in influence by the fertile lowlands of eastern England, a situation which was to remain unchanged until after the Roman period. The uplands of northern Britain and of Ireland were also, more broadly, to lose out to the lowland south in agricultural production. One of the most interesting features of British prehistory is that regions which may be considered marginal today were front-runners in the instigation of social and material changes. Orkney may have been central to the development of henges, Grooved Ware and the new society that they embodied. The earliest evidence of farming, and later for copper tools, is from Ireland. Also, the imprint of settlements and fields in the upland areas of the British Isles may be not simply a relic of changes throughout the whole country, but innovative social developments on relatively underdeveloped land.

The densely wooded landscape of the earliest farmers was transformed over 4000 years of forest clearance and cultivation into an open landscape, which would be more familiar to us if we were able to see it. Many areas remained forested, particularly the heavy clays and the infertile extremities. But the lighter soils had been cleared and, in some areas, ruined for ever. The upland moors, our treasured 'wildernesses' of today, were deforested and their thin soils exhausted and eroded in just a few generations. These may have been the first humanly-contrived ecological disasters, some

3200 years before anyone thought of the green movement.

Archaeologists used to talk of prehistory as a march of progress, bringing these early people out of savagery and barbarism to a state of civilization. The successive ages of stone, bronze and iron were considered proof of this progress by a society which measures technological advancement as the highest goal. There was probably little improvement in people's health between the Neolithic and the Iron Age. Throughout this time, people lived much shorter lives and no doubt endured considerable physical suffering from toothache, rheumatism and broken bones. There is, however, no question that the metal and wood technologies of the end of the Bronze Age were more sophisticated than the stone- and wood-working of earlier times. But skills were lost on the way. Neolithic fencing hurdles from the Somerset Levels were made to a standard that was not maintained in industrial Britain. We are only just rediscovering how these simple technologies can be used to their greatest effect.

These societies were intensely conservative by our standards. There were long periods, spanning tens of generations, when there were few or no innovations. Change, when it came, was often far-reaching and dramatic, though we do not know whether such changes occurred over tens of years or over hundreds. Their view of time was probably completely different to our own. We see the past, the present and the future as parts of a linear sequence. The future for us will be different from the present; we hope for progress. All our evidence for people's experience of time in the Neolithic and Bronze Age points to a concern with cyclical time. In other words, time did not go forwards, from a past to a present, but round and round in the cycles of the sun and moon. In such a scheme, human life would also have been considered to revolve from birth to death to rebirth as ancestral beings who themselves bestowed life. Concepts of linear time were probably only weakly developed and, with no innate view of progress and advancement, innovations would have been viewed with suspicion and distrust. Yet change did occur, either barely perceived as almost insignificant deviations from traditional practices or as sweeping and radical transformations when people did away with many of the old ways and built a new world. This new way of life might then form a great tradition, apparently timeless and possibly lasting for many centuries.

We can identify three great traditions, each replacing the other. Our technological framework of stone (Neolithic) and bronze has obscured these three ages, which may be defined in different terms. The first was the age of the ancestors, when communal tombs were built to consolidate the agricultural expansion and ensure continued fertility. The second age was the age of astronomy when great monuments were built to map the heavens. The third was the age of water cults, when weapons and wealth were destroyed in quantity.

The Age of Ancestors and Tombs

The age of ancestors followed on from that uncertain time when there may have been farming alongside gathering and hunting. It began with the first great onslaught on the forests, no doubt aided by the disease carried by the elm beetle. The fertile and well-drained soils were sought out for cultivation. Life was probably fairly mobile as people exploited river valleys, upland plains and forests. The great symbols of the age were the axe, that instrument of clearance, and the ancestral tomb, in which resided the mingled remains of previous generations who had first staked their claim to new land (116). Across the British Isles, the pottery, tombs and axes formed regional groups that partly overlapped. We do not know whether these regional styles represented social groupings such as different tribes. If so then there may have been up to eight in England alone.

Archaeologists have wondered whether there were chiefs at this time or whether people were relatively equal. Opinion is completely divided. The evidence can be looked at in different ways. The deposits from the causewayed enclosures and tombs suggest that society was divided on the basis of age and by gender; adult males being at the top of society. The tombs and enclosures also required considerable community effort to build. Was there a hidden hand behind each community effort? A hereditary line of leaders? Or was this genuinely a community effort organized by elders of the group or tribe, whose authority was only temporary? The relative status of women may have declined, in Yorkshire, Wessex and Ireland at least, towards the end of this age. The new

116 *Reconstruction of the Street House long barrow, Cleveland.*

emphasis on communal or individual burial of adult men in the funeral monuments and the more conspicuous gender distinctions in dress suggest that women were less valued as social equals. Also by this time, the rate of land clearance slowed down, if not went into reverse. Woodlands regenerated and the more marginal and uncertain farming lands were abandoned. If women's social position had been related to their child-rearing abilities then perhaps the end of expansion indicated that continued peopling of the land was no longer the highest priority. The appearance of fortified enclosures and their subjection to attacks also point to a growing age of uncertainty.

117 *Reconstruction of the Neolithic house at Ballyglass (Co. Mayo).*

The Age of Astronomy and Sacred Landscapes

The next age began probably in Orkney and eastern Ireland. It was an age when the past was invoked to an almost stultifying degree in the present. Enormous monuments were constructed, many of them to chart the passage of the sun and moon (**118**). This was not a time of agricultural expansion or growth and we might interpret it as given over to the vain follies of commemorative architecture. In architectural and technological terms there were great advances: circles of timber and stone, huge mounds (**119**) and long enclosures were constructed across the landscape. As we know from many other societies, it is possible to develop a detailed knowledge of astronomy using the simplest of technology. You do not have to build enormous structures of standing stones and tree-trunks or dig deep and long ditches. Perhaps the real age of astronomical discovery was during the previous millennium when little or no trace of it has survived. Our 'age of astronomy' is thus an age when that knowledge was consolidated and literally set in stone. The monuments were commemorations of past events as much as instruments of measurement.

Some archaeologists have interpreted this age as the time of the first chiefdoms. In the initial phases, the chiefs are inferred only from the complex organization required for the

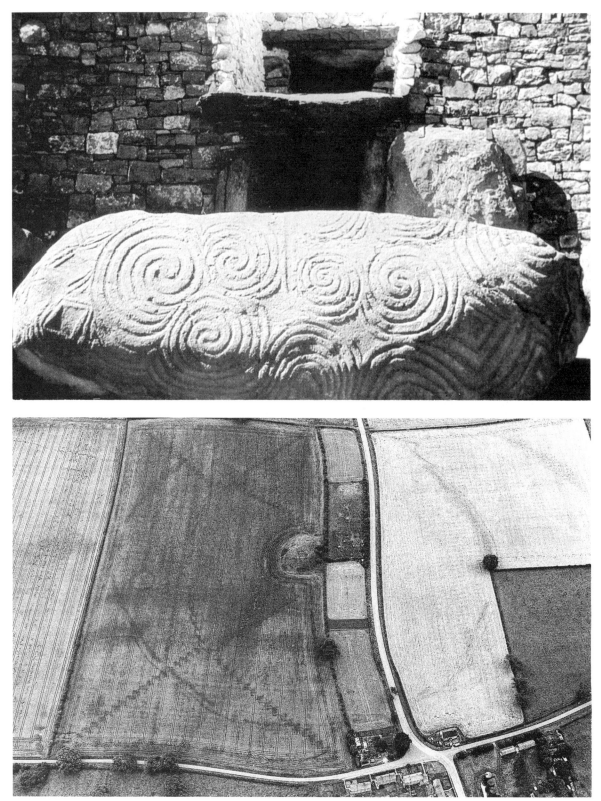

118 (Above left) The entrance of the huge chambered tomb at Newgrange. The lightbox, at the top, and a decorated stone can be seen.

119 (Below left) The large mound at Duggleby Howe (Yorkshire), surrounded by a circular enclosure ditch. The 'envelope' marks in the fields are due to modern crop sowing.

120 A reconstruction of the funerary ceremonies at Irthlingborough.

121 *Reconstruction of the building of Silbury Hill.*

122 *Reconstruction of the cursus at Springfield (Essex).*

construction of the great monuments like Silbury Hill or the earliest stages of Stonehenge. By the later phases, the burials of men with gold and other trappings have been considered to be those of the chiefs themselves. A few barrows were erected over the graves of children, some with quite elaborate grave goods. Again, some archaeologists have taken these to demonstrate hereditary transmission of authority. Since these fancy grave goods are either not particularly abundant or are of types not found in adults' graves, the argument for hereditary authority is weak. People do not bury themselves of course and we have to also picture a grieving parent placing valuables in the grave and organizing the building of a mound over it (**120**). The rich graves of Wessex may have been short-lived as a phenomenon. They probably commemorated the most powerful individuals (or their successors), who had earned their power rather than inherited it. People have suggested that the man in Bush Barrow was the architect of the third stage of Stonehenge. We will never know, but we must remember that the grave goods tell us more

about the mourners than about the person they were buried with. Parts of the landscape were covered by cemeteries of barrows, perhaps expressing people's concerns with their personal and family ancestry (like portraits on a wall in more recent times) rather than with the supernatural powers of ancestors.

This period certainly has its mysteries. Why build the huge mound of Silbury Hill (**121**) in the lowest spot in the landscape? Why was there no burial beneath it? Or did the recent tunnels excavated into it miss any burials within it? What was the link between the hill and the henge at Avebury. How did people use these huge sacred landscapes?

More than any other monuments, the remains from this particular age have elicited considerable fascination from believers in leylines and earth forces. These monuments are taken as indicative of a lost 'Golden Age' with its arcane knowledge of how to live in harmony with the earth and with each other. As commentators have noted of ley-hunters, their vision of the past is founded on a dissatisfaction with the problems of the present. There is also an undercurrent of exclusion by archaeologists of non-professionals from the narrow confines of orthodox academia. There is no doubt that images of a lost wonderland are exceedingly attractive, just as many like to believe in spacemen visiting the earth. The original 'old straight track' theory conceived of straight lines cutting swathes through primeval forest. The 'cursuses' (**122**) might certainly fit that description except that they ran only for a few kilometres at their longest and were built predominantly in already open grassland. Many ley-liners have used simplistic notions of continuity in the landscape, in attempting to align sites of different dates. They have effectively compressed prehistory into a short sequence. As we have seen, there were phases when monuments of the past were reused and embellished; there were also times when these same monuments were abandoned and ignored, sometimes for millennia.

The early farmers lived less in harmony with their environment than did their gatherer-hunter predecessors. They were also wrecking the more vulnerable landscapes. Equally, they were not living in harmony with each other, as the violent deaths from arrow wounds testify. Everyone is entitled to believe what they will, and ley-line beliefs are harmless if also a false

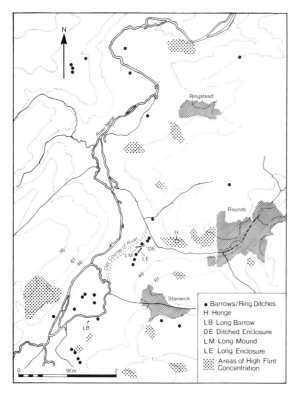

123 *The distribution of Neolithic and Bronze Age monuments and settlement areas in the Nene valley, around Raunds (Northamptonshire). The settlement areas are recognized by dense concentrations of worked flint.*

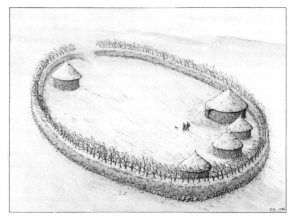

124 *Reconstruction of the settlement of Shaugh Moor.*

They doubtless underestimate the capacity for many individuals in pre-industrial societies to understand the cycles of the sun and moon. When this knowledge is shared amongst the community, there may be no need for such specialists.

The Age of Land Division and Water Cults

From 1700 BC a new order was imposed on the landscape (**125**). The circles, rich burials and sacred landscapes were replaced by land boundaries on an enormous scale. Unfortunately we know little about them in the lowlands except from occasional well-preserved areas like the Fen edge, but the uplands were covered with them. An even greater expenditure of labour went into the construction of these than into the monuments of the previous age. Although fields do not require boundaries of any concrete form, these boundaries, of stone walls or ditches, were imprinted on the landscape. They were virtually permanent and difficult to eradicate in future centuries. This was an era of expansion and there was little reference to distant pasts. Ancient sites were avoided or even slighted by new land boundaries cutting across them.

This was also a time of innovations in metal forms. New axes, larger swords, cauldrons and parade armour were just some of the styles sweeping Europe. The British Isles were

dream. At least such ideas will keep archaeologists on their toes and also prompt them to remember that there is much that is unexplained.

There is also a popular misconception that Stonehenge was built by druids. These Celtic priests were mentioned by Caesar, writing about his invasion of Britain over 1500 years after building works at Stonehenge were abandoned. Their association with Stonehenge is by historical accident. William Stukeley, the eighteenth-century antiquarian, realized that Stonehenge was built before the Roman period but did not appreciate just how long before. He wrongly assumed that, since Stonehenge and druids were pre-Roman, they must have been contemporary. The tradition of druids was probably confined to the Iron Age. In the absence of druids, some archaeologists have talked of a caste or class of astronomer-priests in the later Neolithic and Early Bronze Age.

125 *The layout of the major reave systems on Dartmoor.*

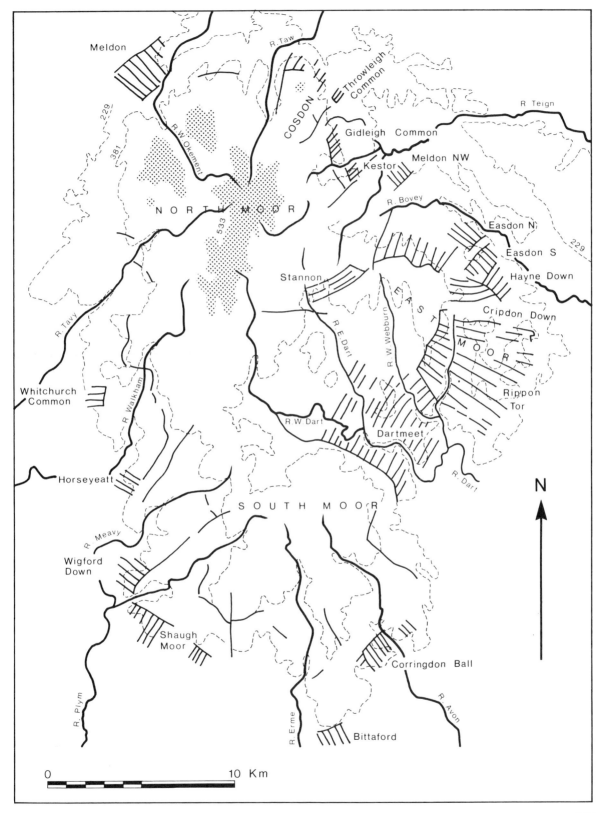

126 *A reconstructed Middle Bronze Age house from Fengate (on display at Flag Fen). It has a roof of turf and reeds. Only the post-holes and eavesdrip gully of the original house survived.*

perched on the very edge of a great European network which extended from Sweden to Spain to Hungary. Within Britain some areas were able to 'plug in' to this network but others were marginalized. The lower Thames and eastern England constituted this core area, trading with the continent. To the west and north were the peripheries. These areas, in Wessex, the Welsh Marches and up into Yorkshire, were poorer in imported metal goods and agricultural production. They were characterized by defended hilltop settlements and may have been subject to raiding and warfare directed out of the core area. The emphasis on fighting and feasting seems to have corresponded with the formation of retinues or armed bands of warriors. There were distinctive territories, marked by different styles of pottery and bronze axes, which pre-figured the Iron Age tribal areas. Each of these may have been controlled by chiefly dynasties or equivalent kinds of autocratic authority. Alternatively, they may have been organized as relatively egalitarian tribal groups. The relative status of women is hard to gauge but they may have become increasingly tied to the settlement compound and the duties of preparing and serving food.

Sites to visit

There are thousands of Neolithic and Bronze Age sites in Britain that can be seen. Most are on private land and can only be visited with the landowner's permission. However, a reasonable number are in public ownership or have some form of public access to them. A few require a payment, but fortunately these are still rare. There is not much in the way of Visitor Centres yet, but two can be singled out which are definitely worth a visit. They are the Flag Fen prehistoric fenland centre in Peterborough (**126**) and the Great Orme mines near Llandudno (see **74**). The small museum at Avebury is worth a visit as part of the Avebury landscape and there are other good collections and displays in the British Museum, the National Museum of Scotland, Devizes Museum, Kirkwall Museum (Orkney), the Irish and Welsh national museums in Dublin and Cardiff, and a whole host of local museums across the country. Useful gazetteers of sites that may be visited can be found in *Exploring Scotland's Heritage*, a series produced by the Royal Commission for Ancient and Historical Monuments of Scotland (published by HMSO), James Dyer's *Penguin Guide to Prehistoric England and Wales* (published in 1981 by Allen Lane) and *Early Ireland: A Field Guide*, by Anthony Weir (published in 1980 by Blackstaff Press). Below is a list of just a few of the monuments and sites mentioned in these gazetteers, principally those where public access is possible or even encouraged. A small number of them are described in booklets, either individually or in groups of sites (such as Orkney), which are available from the various historic monuments commissions. The best general guide for a region is Anna Richie's *Scotland BC*, published in 1988 and available from Historic Scotland.

Southern England

Bant's Carn, Innisidgen and Porthellick Down burial chambers, Isles of Scilly: Some of the many Bronze Age burial chambers on these islands.

Ballowall barrow, St Just, Cornwall: A Bronze Age entrance grave on the edge of a cliff near Land's End, one mile west of St Just.

Hurlers stone circle, Bodmin Moor, Cornwall: Three Bronze Age stone circles, in amongst a relict Bronze Age landscape, half a mile north-west of Minions.

St Breock Downs monolith, Cornwall: A standing stone, probably Bronze Age, which originally stood 5 m (16½ ft) high, nearly 6 km (4 miles) south-south-west of Wadebridge.

Tregiffian chambered tomb, St Buryan, Cornwall: Probably an entrance grave of Bronze Age date, two miles south-east of St Buryan.

Trethevy Quoit, St Cleer, Cornwall: A portal dolmen, probably built in the Early Neolithic, one mile north-east of St Cleer.

Grimspound, Dartmoor: A Later Bronze Age stone-walled enclosure with 24 stone house circles inside, six miles south-west of Moretonhampstead.

Merrivale, Dartmoor: A Later Bronze Age village of stone house circles, close to two stone rows and a burial cist, one mile east of Merrivale. Both these sites are only the tip of an iceberg for Later Bronze Age settlement on the moors.

Upper Plym Valley, Dartmoor: A landscape of stone round houses, field walls (reaves) and cairns, of Bronze Age and possibly Neolithic date, four miles east of Yelverton.

Kingston Russell stone circle, Dorset: A Bronze Age stone circle two miles north of Abbotsbury.

The Nine Stones, Winterbourne Abbas, Dorset: A Bronze Age stone circle a mile and a half west of Winterbourne Abbas.

Maiden Castle, Dorset: A Neolithic causewayed enclosure, bank barrow and Bronze Age round barrow, all within the massive Iron Age ramparts, two and a half miles south-west of Dorchester.

Knowlton henge, Dorset: A henge monument and surrounding Bronze Age barrows a few miles south of the Dorset cursus. There is a ruined Norman church within the henge (three miles west of Cranborne).

Winterbourne Poor Lot barrows, Dorset: A cemetery of 44 round barrows, two miles west of Winterbourne Abbas.

Stanton Drew circles and cove, Avon: A group of three stone circles, two stone rows and a probable Neolithic chamber tomb.

Stoney Littleton long barrow, Avon: A Neolithic chambered tomb within a long mound, one mile south of Wellow.

Uley and Nympsfield long barrows, Gloucestershire: Two Neolithic chambered tombs on the crest of the limestone ridge overlooking the Severn valley. Uley (Hetty Pegler's Tump) requires a torch. The barrows are a couple of miles apart between Nympsfield and Dursley.

Windmill Tump long barrow, Gloucestershire: A chambered Neolithic tomb, south-west of Rodmarton.

Belas Knap long barrow, Gloucestershire: A large Neolithic long barrow, two miles south of Winchcombe.

Notgrove long barrow, Gloucestershire: Another Neolithic chambered tomb, north-west of Notgrove.

Arthur's Stone, Herefordshire: Nothing to do with Arthur; a ruined Neolithic chambered long barrow at Dorstone, seven miles east of Hay on Wye.

Mitchell's Fold stone circle, Shropshire: A Bronze Age stone circle in a dramatic setting, 16 miles south-west of Shrewsbury.

Stonehenge, Wiltshire: A Bronze Age stone circle, a Neolithic cursus and the largest barrow cemetery in Britain.

Durrington Walls and Woodhenge, Wiltshire: Concrete posts mark the postholes of Woodhenge. Look for the enormous ditch and bank of the huge henge, enclosing a small valley next door, just south of Durrington village.

Avebury: A remarkable complex of monuments which includes West Kennet long barrow, Windmill Hill causewayed enclosure, Silbury Hill, Avebury henge (and stone circles), the West Kennet avenue of standing stones, the Sanctuary henge and the excellent Avebury museum, which has been recently redesigned. Do not miss Devizes Museum which has an impressive prehistoric collection.

Whitesheet Hill, Wiltshire: One of the best preserved causewayed enclosures, showing interrupted banks as well as ditches, north of Shaftesbury.

Flowerdown barrows, Littleton, Hampshire: A group of Bronze Age round barrows, two and a half miles north-west of Winchester.

Wayland's Smithy, Uffington, Oxfordshire: An impressive chambered tomb constructed on top of an earlier Neolithic long barrow, a short walk from the White Horse.

The Rollright Stones, Great Rollright, Oxfordshire: A Bronze Age stone circle, a standing stone, a stone burial chamber and a probable long barrow.

Cissbury Ring, near Findon, Sussex: A large Iron Age hillfort sits on the summit but there are traces of Early Neolithic flint mines at the western end of the hill.

Highdown Hill, near Ferring, Sussex: A Late Bronze Age settlement and an Early Iron Age hillfort.

Kit's Coty House and Little Kit's Coty House, Kent: Two ruined Neolithic burial chambers, two miles north of Maidstone.

Grimes Graves, Norfolk: Neolithic flint mines seven miles north-west of Thetford. One of the shafts can be entered to see the galleries.

Flag Fen prehistoric fenland centre, Peterborough: One of the most startling Bronze Age discoveries of recent years. A huge wooden structure preserved underneath the peat is being excavated. There are also reconstructions of prehistoric houses and fields. This is a must!

Northern England

Arbor Low stone circle, Derbyshire: A Later Neolithic henge with a recumbent stone circle inside. Nearby is the Bronze Age barrow at Gib Hill. The sites are two miles south of Monyash.

Nine Ladies stone circle, Stanton Moor, Derbyshire: A Bronze Age stone circle, five miles south-east of Bakewell. There are over 70 Bronze Age barrows and cairns in the area and many of the grave goods are on display in Sheffield Museum.

Mam Tor, Derbyshire: A Late Bronze Age defended hilltop settlement in a popular hiking area at one end of the Pennine Way, four miles west of Hope.

Castlerigg stone circle, near Keswick, Cumbria: A Bronze Age stone circle.

Long Meg and her daughters, Cumbria: A magnificent stone circle. The 4m (13ft) high stone, Long Meg, has cup-and-ring marks.

King Arthur's Round Table and the Mayburgh earthwork, Cumbria: Two henges, at Eamont Bridge, one mile south of Penwith.

Wales

Tinkinswood and St Lythans burial chambers, Glamorgan: Tinkinswood is a striking Early Neolithic burial chamber with a huge capstone. St Lythans ('kennel of the greyhound bitch') is a free-standing stone chamber only a mile away.

Parc le Breos burial chamber, Gower peninsula: A stone-built long barrow with a chamber similar to Notgrove and West Kennet.

Carreg Coetan burial chamber, Dyfed: A portal dolmen on the river Nyfer, near Newport. It was originally covered by a circular cairn.

Capel Garmon burial chamber, Gwynedd: A long barrow with a false entrance and a side entrance, in the upper Conwy valley.

Great Orme mines visitor centre, near Llandudno: A fascinating display of mines which have been exploited, on and off, since the Bronze Age. This is another site that shouldn't be missed.

Anglesey: There are nine Neolithic burial chambers which can be visited on Anglesey (Lligwy, Tregwehelydd, Presaddfed, Trefignath, Bryn Celli Ddu, Bodowyr, Din Dryfol, Ty Newedd and Barclodiad Y Gawres). Bryn Celli Ddu tomb is located inside a henge monument and there is another circular enclosure, dating back to the Neolithic, at Castel Bryn Gwyn. Bronze Age standing stones can be seen at Penrhos Feilw, Ty Mawr and Tregwehelydd. The settlement of round houses on Holyhead Mountain dates, in part, back to the Late Neolithic/Early Bronze Age. There is an excellent guidebook to Anglesey, published by Cadw (the Welsh Historic Monuments Commission).

Scotland

Torhousekie stone circle, Dumfries and Galloway: A circle of recumbent stones with a cairn and standing stones inside it.

Drumtroddan, Dumfries and Galloway: Rock carvings and standing stones.

Cairnholy chambered tombs, Dumfries and Galloway: Two fine Neolithic chambered tombs overlooking Wigtown Bay, four miles south-east of Creetown.

Arran: This island has a number of Neolithic and Bronze Age sites, including chambered tombs at Carn Ban and Torrylin, cairns at Auchagallon and Moss Farm Road, and stone circles on Machrie Moor.

The Kilmartin Valley, Argyll: A complex of prehistoric monuments south of Kilmartin, including a linear cemetery of cairns with a central chambered tomb (Nether Largie South). There are decorated stones in some of the cairns. Nearby are two stone circles at Temple Wood and cup-and-ring carvings at Ballygowan, Baluachraig and other locations.

Cairnpapple Hill, Lothian: A multi-period monument which incorporates a Neolithic cremation cemetery, a henge, a stone circle and a cairn (which can be entered). The hill, near Torpichen, has spectacular views.

Memsie Cairn, Banff and Buchan: A large stone cairn, which was once one of three. It is possible that the stones from the other two were added to it.

Loanhead of Daviot and East Aquhorthies stone circles, Grampian: Two recumbent stone circles. There is a low cairn inside the Loanhead circle.

Tomnaverie stone circle, Grampian: Another recumbent stone circle.

Cullerlie stone circle, Grampian: A curious group of small kerbed cairns within a stone circle, south of Garlogie near Aberdeen.

Corrimony chambered tomb, Inverness: A cairn encircled by standing stones, a few miles east of Cannich, south-west of Inverness.

The Clava cairns, near Inverness: A cemetery of burial cairns, a few miles east of Inverness.

Camster, Hill o' Many Stanes and Cairn o' Get, Caithness: The two chambered cairns of Camster survive in excellent condition. There is another Neolithic chambered tomb at Cairn o' Get. The third site, as its name implies, is a curious set of stone alignments (like a miniature version of the great rows at Carnac in Brittany). The sites are some 15 miles by road south-west of Wick.

Cnoc Freiceadain, Caithness: More Neolithic chambered cairns, eight miles east of Thurso close to Dounreay.

Callanish stone circle, Lewis, Western Isles: A famous stone circle and stone alignments which unusually preceded the construction of a chamber tomb at its centre.

Orkney: These islands have some of the best Neolithic archaeology in Britain but remains of the Bronze Age are largely unknown. Settlements to be seen include Skara Brae, Knap of Howar and now Barnhouse (which is being partially reconstructed). The stone circles of Stenness and Brodgar are near Barnhouse, as is the spectacular tomb of Maes Howe. Other tombs to visit are Cuween, Wideford Hill, Unstan, Quoyness, Holm of Papa Westray South, the bizarre Dwarfie Stane and the collection of tombs spread along the south coast of Rousay (Blackhammer, Knowe of Yarso, Taverso Tuick and Midhowe).

Shetland: Stanydale hall is a large Neolithic building (like the Barnhouse hall) which has smaller houses, field-walls and cairns in its vicinity. The Iron Age broch settlements at Jarlshof and Clickhimin started off as farms in the Late Bronze Age.

Ireland

The Giant's Grave, Burren, Co. Cavan: A fine wedge tomb four miles south of Blacklion village. There is a court tomb at Legalough to the south.

The Burren: A remarkable area of bare limestone which provides the setting for many stone tombs, especially wedge tombs (like Ballyganner South, Baur South, Derrynavahagh and Parknabinnia). There is a portal dolmen at Poulnabrone.

Ballybane, Co. Cork: A cup-and-ring marked stone, six miles south-east of Bantry.

Beenalaght alignment, Co. Cork: A line of six stones in an area with many standing stones, eight miles south-west of Mallow.

Carrigagulla stone circle, Co. Cork: A small stone circle near Ballynagree.

Drombeg, Co. Cork: A stone circle, close to two Iron Age houses and a boiling trough.

Island, Co. Cork: A fine example of a wedge tomb, five miles south of Mallow.

Ardmore, Co. Donegal: A cup-and-ring marked stone, a mile north of Muff.

Beltany, Co. Donegal: A cairn and stone circle, two miles south of Raphoe.

Kilclooney More, Co. Donegal: Two dolmens set within a cairn, four miles north of Ardara. There are other tombs in the vicinity.

Malin More tombs, Co. Donegal: A restored court tomb, a few hundred metres from a group of six stone tombs, two miles southwest of Glencolumbkille.

Shalwy and Croaghbeg, Co. Donegal: Two court cairns in good condition, two miles east of Kilcar.

Derrynablaha, Co. Kerry: A large group of stones decorated with cup-and-ring marks, one mile east of Lough Brin.

Drombohilly Upper stone circle, Co. Kerry: A stone circle, north-east of Lauragh Bridge.

Punchestown, Co. Kildare: A very tall standing stone nearly 7 m (23 ft) high, north of the racecourse.

Shasgar, Co. Leitrim: A court tomb, two miles west of Rossinver.

Tullyskeherny, Co. Leitrim: Two fine court cairns with a good view, three miles southeast of Manorhamilton.

Lough Gur, Co. Limerick: A concentration of prehistoric sites, including stone circles, standing stones, wedge tombs, Neolithic house foundations, two miles north of Bruff.

Proleek portal dolmen, Co. Louth: A good example of a dolmen with a steep roof slab, three miles north-east of Dundalk.

Rockmarshall court cairn, Co. Louth: A large tomb, near Proleek, five miles east of Dundalk.

Aillemore tomb, Co. Mayo: A well-preserved court cairn, five miles south-west of Louisburgh.

Ballyglass tomb, Co. Mayo: An excavated court cairn, underneath which were remains of a Neolithic wooden house.

Bend in the Boyne, Co. Meath: A spectacular complex of tombs, henges and other monuments. The large tombs of Dowth, Knowth and Newgrange are impressive. The reconstructed facade of Newgrange is not to all tastes but communicates the impact of its construction in the Neolithic.

Loughcrew, Co. Meath: Another passage grave cemetery spread over two hills. Many of the original tombs have disappeared from the landscape.

Tara, Co. Meath: This Iron Age ceremonial site includes the 'Mound of the Hostages', originally a Neolithic passage grave.

Carrickglass, Co. Sligo: An impressive portal dolmen, a mile south of Lough Nasool.

Carrowkeel Co. Sligo: A spread out passage grave cemetery in the Bricklieve Mountains, two miles north of Ballinafad.

Carrowmore, Co. Sligo: Another passage grave group, dominated by the large 'Queen Maeve's Cairn', two miles south-west of Sligo.

Creevykeel, Co. Sligo: An excellent example of a double court cairn with two joining forecourts forming an enclosed area.

Deerpark tomb, Co. Sligo: Also known as Magheraghanrush, this court cairn is four miles east of Sligo.

Ashleypark, Co. Tipperary: A burial mound of the Linkardstown group, enclosing a stone chamber, which contained the bones of an old man and a child who died around 3500 BC. This impressive tomb is five miles north of Nenagh.

Baltinglass Hill, Co. Wicklow: A group of five Neolithic tombs with fine views, a mile north-east of Baltinglass.

Rathgall, Co. Wicklow: An Iron Age hillfort which was first inhabited in the Late Bronze Age, three miles east of Tullow.

Dooey's Cairn, Co. Antrim: A Neolithic stone tomb, east of Long Mountain near Dunloy.

Craig's dolmen and Broadstone, Co. Antrim: A portal dolmen, three miles north of Rasharkin, and a cairn half a mile away.

Ballylumford dolmen, Co. Antrim: This portal dolmen stands in someone's front garden at Island Magee.

Navan Fort, Co. Armagh: A large circular earthwork enclosure, off the A28 west of Armagh, the first phase of which was constructed in the Late Bronze Age.

Ballymacdermot Cairn, Co. Armagh: A Neolithic tomb in a beautiful mountain setting, near Bernish viewpoint.

Ballykeel dolmen, Co. Armagh: A portal dolmen at the west foot of Slieve Gullion.

Giant's Ring, Co. Down: A prehistoric enclosure with a stone tomb in the centre.

Ballynoe stone circle, Co. Down: An oval mound surrounded by a circle of standing stones, south of Downpatrick. The mound contains cists and covers a stone cairn. This is a unique site and probably dates to the Later Neolithic and Early Bronze Age.

Legananny dolmen, Co. Down: A photogenic portal dolmen, four miles south of Dromara with good views of the Mourne Mountains.

Goward dolmen, Co. Down: A portal dolmen known as 'Pat Kearney's Big Stone', east of Hilltown.

Drumskinny stone circle, Co. Fermanagh: A stone circle with a cairn and stone alignment, four miles north of Kesh.

Knockoneill tomb, Co. Derry: A well-preserved Neolithic court-tomb reused as a Bronze Age circular cairn and burial site, two miles west of Swatragh.

Beaghmore stone circles, Co. Tyrone: Seven stone circles, nine stone rows and a number of cairns form an intriguing Early Bronze Age monument, on the fringe of Sperrins.

Creggandevesky tomb, Co. Tyrone: A recently excavated court tomb, near Creggan west of Pomeroy round the south shore of Lough Mallon.

Knockmany passage tomb, Co. Tyrone: The tomb has been given a modern covering to protect its 'passage grave art'. The chamber can be entered on summer weekend afternoons. The tomb is two miles north-west of Augher on a hilltop in Knochmany Forest.

Further reading

Barrett, John and Richard Bradley (eds.) 1980, *Settlement and Society in the British Later Bronze Age*, British Archaeological Reports (British Series) 83, Oxford.

Barrett, John, Richard Bradley and Martin Green 1991, *Landscape, Monuments and Society: the Prehistory of Cranborne Chase*, Cambridge University Press, Cambridge.

Barrett, John and Ian Kinnes (eds.) 1988, *The Archaeology of Context in the Neolithic and Bronze Age: Recent Trends*, University of Sheffield, Sheffield.

Bradley, Richard 1984, *The Social Foundations of Prehistoric Britain: Themes and Variations in the Archaeology of Power*, Longman, London.

Burgess, Colin 1980, *The Age of Stonehenge*, Dent, London.

Burl, Aubrey 1983, *Prehistoric Astronomy and Ritual*, Shire, London.

Burl, Aubrey 1987, *The Stonehenge People*, Dent, London.

Clarke, David, Trevor Cowie and Andrew Foxon 1985, *Symbols of Power at the Time of Stonehenge,* National Museum of Antiquities of Scotland, Edinburgh.

Coles, Bryony and John Coles 1986, *Sweet Track to Glastonbury: the Somerset Levels in Prehistory*, Thames & Hudson, London.

Coles, John and Anthony Harding 1979, *The Bronze Age in Europe: An Introduction to the Prehistory of Europe c.2000–700 BC*, Methuen, London.

Fleming, Andrew 1988, *The Dartmoor Reaves: Investigating Prehistoric Land Divisions*, Batsford, London.

Harbison, Peter 1988, *Pre-Christian Ireland, from the First Settlers to the Early Celts*, Thames & Hudson, London.

Hedges, John 1984, *Tomb of the Eagles: a Window on Stone Age Tribal Britain*, John Murray, London.

Jones, Martin 1986, *England before Domesday*, Batsford, London.

Mercer, Roger 1980, *Hambledon Hill, a Neolithic Landscape*, Edinburgh University Press, Edinburgh.

O'Kelly, Michael 1989, *Early Ireland: an Introduction to Irish Prehistory*, Cambridge University Press, Cambridge.

Saville, Alan 1990, *Hazleton North. The Excavation of a Neolithic Long Cairn of the Cotswold–Severn Group*, English Heritage Archaeological Report, No. 13, London.

Thomas, Julian 1991, *Rethinking the Neolithic*, Cambridge University Press, Cambridge.

Wainwright, Geoffrey 1990, *Henges*, Thames & Hudson, London.

Related books in the Batsford/English Heritage series

Malone, Caroline 1989, *Avebury*.

Pryor, Francis 1991, *Flag Fen: Prehistoric Fenland Centre*.

Richards, Julian 1991, *Stonehenge*.

Sharples, Niall 1991, *Maiden Castle*.

Index

INDEX